THE MAN NAMED EAST

By Peter Redgrove

The Collector and Other Poems
Routledge & Kegan Paul

The Nature of Cold Weather and Other Poems
Routledge & Kegan Paul

At The White Monument and Other Poems
Routledge & Kegan Paul

The Force and Other Poems
Routledge & Kegan Paul

Work in Progress (Poems 1969)

The Hermaphrodite Album (with Penelope Shuttle)

Dr Faust's Sea-Spiral Spirit and Other Poems
Routledge & Kegan Paul

In the Country of the Skin
Routledge & Kegan Paul

The Terrors of Dr Treviles: A Romance
(with Penelope Shuttle)
Routledge & Kegan Paul

Sons Of My Skin: Redgrove's Selected Poems 1954-74
Routledge & Kegan Paul

The Glass Cottage: A Nautical Romance
(with Penelope Shuttle)
Routledge & Kegan Paul

From Every Chink of the Ark and Other New Poems
Routledge & Kegan Paul

The Wise Wound (with Penelope Shuttle)

The God of Glass: A Morality
Routledge & Kegan Paul

The Weddings at Nether Powers and Other New Poems
Routledge & Kegan Paul

*The Sleep of the Great Hypnotist: The Life and Death
and Life After Death of a Modern Magician*
Routledge & Kegan Paul

The Beekeepers: A Novel
Routledge & Kegan Paul

The Apple-Broadcast and Other New Poems
Routledge & Kegan Paul

The Man Named East
and other new poems

Peter Redgrove

ROUTLEDGE & KEGAN PAUL
London, Boston, Melbourne and Henley

First published in 1985
by Routledge & Kegan Paul plc
14 Leicester Square, London WC2H 7PH, England
9 Park Street, Boston, Mass. 02108, USA
464 St Kilda Road, Melbourne,
Victoria 3004, Australia and
Broadway House, Newtown Road,
Henley-on-Thames, Oxon RG9 1EN, England
Set in Baskerville
by Columns, Reading
and printed in Great Britain
by St Edmundsbury Press Ltd
Bury St Edmunds, Suffolk

Library of Congress Cataloging in Publication Data

Redgrove, Peter.
The man named East, and other new poems.
I. Title.
PR6035.E267M3   1985   821'.914   84-17710

ISBN 0-7102-0014-5 (pbk.)

Dedicated to G.M., whose writings have been
a source of inspiration for more than a decade,
and to S.M., *fons chymicae veritatis*.

Contents

Preface   xi
Call   1
In the Pharmacy   2
The Heart   3
Redecorations   4
Falmouth at its Best   5
The Green Tower   5
Killing House   7
Pub Signs   9
The Quiet Woman of Chancery Lane   9
The Cornish Kiss   11
Feast of the Pisculi   12
Under the Duvet   14
Cornwall Honeymoon   16
The Effigies   17
Shells   18
The Work of Water   20
Warfare   22
To the Water-Psychiatrist   23
The Proper Halo   25
The Party in the Woods   27
The Funeral   30
Paper Door   31
Warm Stone for N   33
Mother Kheb   35
The Drumming Stars   36
An Egyptian Requiem   37
The Sister in the Glass   39
Assembly   41
The Grain-Shaped Cave   43
Musk   44
Moth on Globe   46

Contents

Unpasteurized	47
National Trust	48
Transactions	49
Lights in the Mist	50
Cloudmother	51
Mothers	53
Customs	54
A Ghost Sonata	55
The Man from Selborne	56
Censer Mountain	57
The Will of November	58
She Believes she has Died	59
The College in the Reservoir	60
The Man Named East	61
A Kinsman	63
Lesson on the Banjo	64
In Autumn Equinox	66
Seaside Clinic	67
Diva	69
Whitsunwind	71
Rusty Breath	72
Soft Handling	73
Fetish	75
The Brothel in Fairyland	76
Mothers and Child	78
The Pale Brows of Lightning	80
Like a Rock	82
In Norwich Museum	83
Too Old for Bones	85
The Invisible Man & Co.	87
Word	89
The Wheel	91
Wooden Wheat	93
The Comforter	95
Serpent of the Month Club	97
Light Black Redskin	98
Yoga Cronies	100
Seiza	101
The Alchemical Honeymoon	103
The Young and Pregnant Spiritualist	105

Contents

Duessa   106
The Witch Who Loves Us   108
The Reason Why Witches Wear Black   109
Air   110
Tantric Friends   112
Flow and Fold   114
City of Boys   115
Butchers   117
The Ghost-Bomb Kiss   118
Presences   119
And He Causeth Souls to Shine   120
Town and Country   122
Another You   124
Working Window   126
The Ships   127
The Offices in the Old Baths   129
The Harmony   133

Preface

Grateful acknowledgments are due to the following magazines and anthologies in which certain of the poems first appeared: *Descant, Encounter, Equivalencías, Gallimaufry, The Greenfield Review, The Literary Review, The Living Poet* (BBC), *The London Magazine, The London Review of Books, The Manhattan Review, New Poetry 8* (Arts Council), *The Observer, Outposts, Oxford Poetry, Poetry Book Society Supplement 1982, Poetry Review, Poems for Poetry 84, The Scotsman, Spectrum, South West Review, Sulfur, Temenos, Tenfold* (Poems for Frances Horovitz), *Three Spires Festival Programme 84, The Times Literary Supplement, Two Plus Two*.

Particular thanks are due to the Editors of *Equivalencías* (Summer-Autumn 1982), *The Manhattan Review* (vol. 2, no. 2 and vol. 3, no. 1) and *Poetry Review* (vol. 71, nos 2-3) for their special supplements; and to Taxus Press for its pamphlet *The Working of Water*.

CALL
(*For F*)

The shipwright's beauty, who butchers the forest,
Dresses it again in shining sails,

Garments like blossom,

And nailed with new iron like budding grain,
With big ship-bosoms full of wonderful fruit
And men of unbelievable expertise
Of knowledge of the stars and sands;

You serve branching ocean routes
As though the whole sea were a sailing-tree
And the ships were blossom on it
Gliding slowly
On its world-embracing boughs
Transferring goodness and prosperity,

You give them yare names:
Ocean Moon, Tidesource,
And their travellers a berth of womb
In the big-belly blown along
By blinding blossom;

And others dig
And uncover the scarlet iron
And with fire forge sounding hulls and bells
And the great mines of iron feather on the waters,
The heaviest stone sails the wide seas,

1

Or in the dusty dry dock
Resounds to its remaking
As a cathedral calls out to its glad city to serve.

IN THE PHARMACY
For Wendy Taylor

A moth settled on the side of a bottle,
Covering its label, a marvel. The embroidered wings
Of the moth called Wood Leopard. It flutters off

And settles on another bottle. The label of this violet
Fluted container with the glass stopper reads
Lapis invisibilitatis: it would make you disappear.

The moth like a travelling label walks
From bottle to marble bottle with floury wings
Embracing each and tapping with fernleaf tongue

Sugared drops at neck and stopper,
Built like a fat rabbit with gaudy wings extracting
The essence of pharmacies, the compendium,

Staggering from jar to sculptured jar and sealing
Into capsules its own cogitatio,
Implicating in its eggs our explicit medicine.

And the draughts of invisibility, the poisons?
The caterpillar remembers to die, and disappears,
As the labelled stone declares,

All melts to caterpillar soup inside the wrappings
Where the pupa cogitates,
Just the nerve-cord floating like a herring-skeleton,

And round those nerves lovingly unfolds
The nervous wings on which is marked
In beautiful old pharmacy script, the formula.

THE HEART

An autumn bluebottle,
Frail winged husk with the last squeezings
Of the year sealed up inside,

The last juices and saps of the fruits
Crystallising inside the stone gaze
Of the insect-mask, countenance of sugars.

It sings softly, in search of sugars.
The maiden sings softly,
She whose red blouse

Is blowing on the line,
Its buttons glittering like sugar,
Full of the wind's tits,

That I saw her filling yesterday;
As though she had given one of her bodies
To the elements,

For the weather to fill,
The red blouse pulsing on the line,
Emptying and filling like a heart

In the strong gusts,
The wind's heart beating on the line;
And the sails of blood,

The stout red-rigged yachts competing on the estuary,
Red for celerity and heart,
And the transparent word breathing everywhere.

The maiden and the fly sing softly,
It butts its drumstick head against her window,
She stares out at a heart of hers beating in the weather,

The fly so full of low sweetness it hums like rubbed crystal.

REDECORATIONS

A few skilful touches, deft licks of the brush,
Our bathroom changed to a high pavilion over the estuary
With its water-throne, and its reclining water-sofa
And the plump sudsing scatter-cushions.

She walked in a rainy cloud of silks;
She replied in a soft and cultured voice
That she would soon be nineteen.

She got into the bath and disappeared
Behind the crystal curtains to the shower.
The odours of many gardens came through those curtains.

I peeked to see if there were gardens there;
I saw her shaking her sleeves of water.

Restored thus, we descended.

The clergy were in their drinking-clothes
(Our grounds are connected by a small gate)
He wore a kind of cricketer's lily-nostril of the heart:
His shirt rose to a high collar and broke open in front.

FALMOUTH AT ITS BEST

The crew of a submarine
Buying jewellery in the town.
The dusk shepherd
Leading his flock to water just outside it.
A man with a liver-coloured face
Flopped in the sawdust of a butcher's shop.

Under the corrugated iron roof,
The cinema's elastic shadows lean forward and snap back.

The pyramid with the flush strongroom door
Is a memorial to the squires, it peaks
Taut to the horizon-line,
The sleek horizon-line.

There's always a small piece of shit lying outside the
    magistrate's entrance.

The trigger of the sun
Shoots my shadow out in front.
The sea's on edge.
It is full of submarines, transporting jewellery.

Keep the line sleek to catch the fish.

A banquet on a flower-boat
Out on the Roads; fishing in their silks
The good companions, taut, angular and sleek.

THE GREEN TOWER
(*Carn Brae*)

Leaves on their wooden shelves
Like shelf after shelf of shiny footgear
All marching on the wind,

5

Boots without soldiers,
The battleground of wind
Under one blue helmet,

Spirit soldiers marching in their winged boots,
The sycamore of the churchyard full of ghost
By this broad calm church

Light and airy and white with plain windows,
Built in the seventeen hundreds
Like a rational cabinet of light and praise

And at the nave-back a step down into an old tower,
The old bell-tower with the map of scores of churches
All the bell-able churches in Cornwall.

As I stepped down into this area
I thought that a high bell must still be ringing,
Have lately been rung,

Or its late echoes were caught still in the crystals
Of the dark stone blocks of this elder tower,
And like an electricity a slight

And relaxing current passed through my whole skin
And I stepped out into the broad church and there was
    nothing
And I stepped back into the stone tower that was tingling

And I stepped out and took her back down with me
And she felt it also, like the near presence of water.
And outside the tall tower was green from weather,

And with its gargoyles that looked like piskies of the rain,
Like a towering haunt of piskies, the green tower;
And every Sunday the tiger of blood

Lashed its tail on their altar,
The bible turned its pages
Over and over not wearing them out,

The souls all marched in the big
Thumping boots of their hymns,
The congregation roaring aloud with their cunning

Who have that sweet relenting pagan
Bell-hung current at their Cornish back.

KILLING HOUSE

I

Creates a haunted house
By filling it with dead folk; the church
A haunted killing-house of graves

That gathers all ghosts with its one death,
One continuous death
That has lasted roughly 2000 years so far,

The same death in all the churches simultaneously,
A death from which ghost issues ceaselessly.
There are rolling rivers

Of all the houseless secular ghosts
Like mists created by the dying leaves,
Like the white rivers of Par,

Like wooded hills that blow fanfares of ghosts
On the night wind as the moon rises.
It houses them.

II

God must be naked
Since we remove our clothes to create souls,
We pass the ghost shuddering from person to person

As one would hang an impossible suspension,
A perilous shaking bridge like the impossible thing
Everlastingly done in church,

Killing and eating the god that cannot die
Which creates much ghost;
And that other world breaks through

Crying in Christ's voice for Mama;
The women making themselves up and perfuming themselves,
Charging themselves with ghost,

Opening their naves,
Gardeners and flowers in one,
Haunted gardens of the future children

Who pluck as they arrive the red flowers.
An aeroplane scratches the high sky with steam;
Like a child in a haunted house

We rub the windowpane to catch a glimpse,
We desire to watch a thing which is not ghost.
If you are not baptised in church

God does not know your name
To call you unto Him,
It was not said out loud

Into his vaulted ear, and with this fright
They drive the ghosts back year after year
Woolbacks stiff with threat unto their shepherd

Before the Cross where unthinkable things occur,
The crossing of the wooden bridge
By the nails in it, the haunted

Bleeding footbridge dangling at nave's end.

PUB SIGNS
(*For G.M.*)

The Veiled Woman has grown flesh over her face
Like a smooth grapeskin, next door
To the modeller of the young in clusters,

The Queen Vine. The liberty men from 'Tidesource'
Drink at *The Half Moon*, and the boards painted
With *The Big Dipper* creak in the polar wind

Past *The Pole Star*, that unmoving source,
And the mutton-leg of *The Seven Stars*,
For such are the benefits flowing from her thigh,

She stands, *The Good Woman*, with her head gone,
The Quiet Woman who is *The Headless Duchess*,
And *The Tall Woman* with her drinkers so relaxed

They know themselves to be likewise of that stature,
Even in *The Straw Threshold* which signifies
The grain threshed out to make the drink,

And as women who have produced are said to be
'In the straw', one may see
By *The Crowned Child* how *The Mother's Veil*

Skins off the daughter's newborn bareface.

THE QUIET WOMAN OF CHANCERY LANE

The blind girl points at a star.
At night, she says, when all the stars are out,
She feels their rays feathering on her face,
Like a fringe of threads.

She stands by the beehive's low thunder.
There will be snow, the bees of ice
Will swarm from their darkening hives. I see

Clouds are gliding, and becoming, in the moonlight,
Mountaineering from nowhere, as the mass of air,
The town's hanging breath, soars into the cold
And is ice in dirigible bergs
And apparitions of a terrain they have created:
Cloudscape. How, under these glories, I wonder

Can men stroll past in deadblack suits, signifying
Ignorance and blindness of the skin,
Swinging griefcases packed with inky briefs,
And a spring in their step from this uniform?
They have a blind confidence, she says, in their power
And in the courts cry 'Proof, proof!',
They can make all others' skins go sightless,

Blind with worry, yet mine, she says,
The Quiet Woman without eyes,
Not living in my head,
The Headless Woman, my skin
Is open as the night sky, with the remote stars
And nearer glories easing across; my eyes
Are blind, but I know these people
By the no-shapes of their numbness as they go,
But since, blind, I am not in their power,
Being afflicted by God, they will not touch me,

With their penal pleading, for I belong
To Another, Who has my eyes. These lawful men
To her are like stars that have gone black, turned
Inside out with the suction of nothingness,
Empty sockets walking the Inns of Court.

The blind girl points to the stars
As if she could see; she informs me
How a special breath from space
Tells her they are out in their moist fullness.

Yet the sky is so packed, how can she not,
Pointing, light on some constellation or other?

But I believe her when she tells me how
Her life without eyes is so full. I take
The blind girl by her night hand.
With her fingers raised, she traces in the air
The slow rising of that mountain that hangs, the full moon,

It is like the presence of a fountain, she says,
Like the fresh aura of falling water, or like
That full head of the thistle I stroked in the park,
And its sound is like a fountain too, or like snow thistling.

THE CORNISH KISS

The hard dark feathery cases of beetles
Like black fingernails.
They fly balancing these cases

Like shining fingernails
Clickering.
A swing on a tree, flying;

The upwards thrill into knowledge.
A kiss that calls current upwards
As if I were some electrical machine,

Some storage battery of brine and leather.
A bird flutters in the throat.
Resonance, resonance, even the knives and forks

Clinking silver of Cornish mines,
The hill of mines with a great beard of pebbles
Through which the white torrents run,

Bands and segments come looping.
A daffodil sensation, as if
Like a parasol the penis opened and shut.

The marsh full of spirits swarming like flies,
Glittering,
And the dogshit embossed with these jewels

For the duration of this kiss.
The opening of pores
To give forth persuasion and affection.

An aerial tunic like a cobweb, the churchplace
Full of gossamer and a wind like beating wings
Which fevers the gossamer.

A glittering mud packed with purpleblack beetlecases
Relaxed beyond endurance.

FEAST OF THE PISCULI
(*Honeymoon County*)

This glass of beer
Like an amber portal,
A crest on the label:
The Beetlegod portrayed
Crouched at a potter's wheel
Forming the Egg.
Beetle's Beers.
Can everything be saved?

The eiderdown begins beating
Like the memories of wings,
For the *homme fait* whose years
Are triaded by tens,
His flight in bed
Towards what?

12

Which is not Christian, his shadow
Going before him, his helpful
Shadow, protecting him, his stiff
Covering shade, and

Sliding down the girl's face
A long convoy of tears
Shining like lorries through the night,
Thick warm tweed from her back
Hitched over the chair,
The silent suit of heath,
The plaits and diadems of tweed,

Their Christian life
Brought down to Cornwall
In jeopardy,
Can anything be saved?
In Merlin's sea-cave
The stalactites all began dripping as
(He watched astounded)
The Moon rose.
They passed in warm tweed
Over the cliff heath through glittering web.

The shewings
Were for the Pisculi,
The Little Fishes,
The first Christians,
We must not expect it
Nowadays, the child
Celebrated at the solstice,
I'll drink to that,
The man at the equinox,
And I'll drink to that too, who
Demonstrated his solar nature
By walking on the waters at dawn.

How then should the piskie
Squat at the centre
Of the web

Shaking it with laughter,
The spider her wolfhound,
The beetle her cat?
But the miracle is
The eiderdown begins
Again to beat, a feathery portal,

And this time she does not cry
Unhusked of tweed
Being in possession of a Silent Body
Where the Lord
Of the Silent Body presides
At the rising of the Moon
In its body of silence,

And what if he enters from the bottle?
A unity appears like an amber
Web through the body
Who shall disclaim it
In this cave of the Pisculi
Which is a wedding-feast
Of the silent bodies
In the auspices of the Amber Portal
In Cornwall not despicable

Their eiderdown like the one goosewing
Of the world, beating.

UNDER THE DUVET

Sleep-feather, the sleep-feather
Comes drifting down,
Rocking the child to sleep,

The child sleeps covered
In a bag of drifting sleep-feathers;
Eider-plume, the ducks are flying

14

Loftily through feathered clouds.
She sleeps flying through their death,
Their flow of plumage, bag of the whole flock.

Just as we realise with care
That we are dreaming, just there,
Entering the Self, and leaving, just there,

That we are asleep, and watching a dream,
And just there, waking, but entering
The small door of a second, the opening of a tick,

The nip of a cog, and watching,
Our Mother above shakes out her bag and the snow flies,
Or the dew manifests; like stars

They are suddenly there, a multitudinising of the grasses,
A heavying and a lighting-up,
We glance down, and the dew is there,

Like all the still seconds
There ever were, stopped,
Each one seeing into the morning, deep

In the interior of its glance, the morning;
And it is a dream of feathery embrace
Like a cloud pluming a mountain,

And the fleeces of sheep too heavy to walk,
So they must settle, and sleep
As the cloud settles

Grazing the mountain, among the silvered grass
Where all, air, mountain, sheep
Is a feathered being, silent with fog,

And within a fleeced pinion
I see the dark mouth of a cave
And enter the cavern

And am immediately among
A feathering of echoes
And I remember that Goddess

Who hid her child to conceal his cries,
Hid him in a cave known for winding passages
And galleries among which the echoes

Never ceased to cry, and surely
This is the passage along which the cloud retires
To its mountain's interior in the daytime,

To its inner pasture, and I find
That my hair and my dress
Are plumed with that cloud's dew

As the spiderwebs and the grasses are feathered
On every fibre with the water
Of the mountain's grey brain ever-distilling

Among its cool granite convolutions,
And I squeeze droplets out of my sleeve
On to my lips, the cloth is rough and the taste

Is of cloth, sheep, grass, wings and ancient water
Stilled over and redistilled until it shines
Again like the plumage

Birthwet from its egg of the newborn angel.

CORNWALL HONEYMOON

Kaolin. A white shadow
Spread across half a county. All the streams
Flaming white. The soil packed

Underfoot solid with light. A beach
With drifts of dead leaves instead of pebbles.
Flowering fogs and the cold fur of moths.

The waves curl and dry,
Leave lines of tiny shells, the fruits
Of the spent waves. After the bath

She blazed with beauty. The crane of the docks
Like a fire-escape to heaven, a staircase
Of steel into the sky, I will see it

Magnificently wreathed in ivy. The eyes
Meeting in orgasm, the salty breath exchanged,
The kaolin waters of the man and woman mingling,

They have ascended the wreathed staircase completely.

THE EFFIGIES

Statues white from the cutting-machine,
Freshly-cut statues white as camellias

By the glassworks which is great corrugated sheds
Of windows rearing on the point
That flash the sun as the windows close and open
And roll out great panes of new glass
Sliding scenery sideways

By the stone-cutting sheds white as mills
With their flour of rock, their effigy-dust,
The petal-white fresh statues sliding from the dark machine.

Cutting the effigies creates
Supple white shadows that line the sheds
The hollow smoke of a statue shaped
For an instant by what has been taken from it
By fast and sparkling wheels of knives,

(Effigy-shadows, white as the full water-shades of the
    sun-god)

And the milk-coloured streams full of excess statue
Come sliding out under the doors
Where you could take workers fright-white with effigy-dust
For clowns or statues; come

Let us put this one back into the machine;

Some we put back again and again
With many passages of copious smoke
Concentrating them, small as a rain-drop or wheat-grain;

Or in life-sized ranks, held still in the landscapes of new glass.

SHELLS

See shells only as seawater twining back
To the first touch, of seawater on itself;

The water touching itself in a certain way,
With a certain recoil and return, and the mollusc

Starts up in the water, as though the conched wave
Had been struck to stone, yet with the touch

Still enrolled in it, the spot was struck
And life flooded through it

Recording a thin stone pulse of itself,
Its spiral photo-album, its family likeness

Caught in nacreous layers, as if
Your skull grew spiring from a skull-button,

Your roles coiling out of your smallest beginning;
Full of shelves of selves

Turning around each other
Like a white library that has been twisted,

Like a spired library turned in the tornado
Unharmed, keeping the well of itself

Open to past and future,
Full, like the mollusc, of the meat of sense,

The briny meat, twirled by the tornado;
And this, whose fleshy books have swum away,

Emptying the magnificent pearl-building,
All its walls luminous in the sunlight,

Empty stairwell full of sound,
For since the books created the shelves

To fit their message and their likeness,
Echoes of books remain, resounding,

Printed endlessly around the shelving,
Like the seasound of seapages turning over

And over, touching themselves
In a certain way, echoing, reminding,

Evoking new themes of old sea-shapes. A new shell,
A new skull begins again from its speck

Echoing the older books made of water.
See how the clouds coil also above the eggshells of cities,

Touching each other in certain ways, so that
Rain falls; clouds invisible

Over the sea, but when the watery air
Lifts over the land, the white shells float

Crystallised over the hot cities, muttering with thunder.

THE WORK OF WATER

A water-psychiatrist: the plumber
Who has agreed to call
At any emergency
So that I need never fear
I can't give my head a good wash
At any time, a good sluice.
The waterworks is my secure castle,
My water-rock of ages, my silver tower,
My moon on earth;

Waterfortress
With battlements and keep and portcullis,
And, filling it, one silver friend,
A soldier, who breaks over my head
In armies, at command;

The silver squads
Flowing to the tunes of pipes,
Or camping in the works
And drumming in the pumps;
One big silver soldier
Standing at attention in cisterns,

Stilling soldier; and in the frost
The claws and laces of his armour,
The swords he slashes everywhere!

The great stillicide
Of all the faucets of the drops
That enclose us quite, each of us laid out
In his waterbathdrop sentry-box;

Spin the tap
And the great sluice glides up
Far away in some defile,
Replacing troops that spend themselves down here
Mobbing us with glittering arms;

The soldier who is deep green
In his native river, and pushes with his shoulder
Over the weirs where their buttresses
Build water up to shine against the sky
In locks controlled by taps like steering-wheels;
And the drilling pipes
Feeding at the still green pits
And glittering trenches parade him
So I see myself shining in these boots and belts;

And the tan tavern, the tap, the tabard
With the tapster? Fill the inn with water!

Fill the church with water!
Let those old stones be our Works
With the Waves flowing across the altar at us,
Foaming into surplices, drink it
As it freshly flows, like a kiss
Of a great and powerful Waterperson
Soldiering through us.

WARFARE

Dwelling in a house of chintz
Like a petrific Indian Summer;
Visions become sleep.

The fabrics take their photos;
That's that.
The printed tendrils suck at the living scenes.

The tall woman with the rangy step
Strides back through the foliage,
She is a design, serving clouded tea.

The pot-pourri,
That mummified garden,
Gives off its sensuals in slow-motion,

As grey shell after shell
Is cast off by my bonfire,
Shaken off, shell after shell,

Like the leafy canopies shed
Over and over in re-enactment,
The very prints of autumn

And its spices; then the wind drops,
The being grows rangy,
Half-lucent ghost,

Coiling head striped with sunbars,
A gigantic dilute genie
In his autumn-smelling robes,

Balanced on the point
Of his small concentrated bottle,
Balancing tip-toe in his flame,

Pungent ghost, breath-snatcher,
Brilliant garden of scent
With grey admixture;

To the nose a landscape pouring up,
Shadowing the lawn with a tree,
Towering with imaginations!

I should put to the flame
The chintz house,
Its tendrils would coil,

Its scenes race,
In fires the women vault
With scorched valances

Sneezing and high-laughing
Alive as warfare to which the horse
Whinnies, Ha!

TO THE WATER-PSYCHIATRIST

I

The water-psychiatrist: the plumber
Who will come at my emergency,
So that I can give my head another good wash.

Mice, porcupines, sloths and shrews:
All the same core-mammal, the obsession
Of all species, the family face,

So different from antelopes who are
Skittish as butterflies, leaping wise-faced
Like an astronaut at the end of his silken string.

In the gurgle of the urinal
I took a charge of water-electricity
Straight through the end of my penis;

The cistern was discharging with a white noise,
The cleanly electrix went right up my tube
(Now I have something to tell my plumber)

Leaping like that antelope through my mouse,
A charge right down from the waterworks
And through the fresh green hill of springs

Where the deer leap, bounding over streams,
Down from the clouds fluttering with lightning.
I shimmered with electrocution harmlessly,

With urinal lightning in the beer-smells
Enriched like a boudoir by gathering, in their passage,
All the perfumes of the magic galleries

They had passed through, drinking up
The pictures of thought painting themselves
And repainting over the red walls, enriched

Like the balsamic inside canopy of a great tree.

II

(Then there is the pacing puddle of her shiny shirt;
Her way of slapping together a cheese sandwich:
As she does it a figure of lancing light
Flashes across her shirt-back;

This shock went up my generation also;
I became skittish; the antelope
Of light was in the shirt; my mouse ran;
I was a hedgehog with prickles in my skin.)

24

III

I went out resolving to trace the source.
The little stream rippling down the hillside
Entered the urinal, so I travelled up

The glittering electrical water I had felt in my generations
(Some lightning flashed into a tarn held in the hilltop?)
Towards the source. It was a spring

Overarched by a tree, the source had reduced
The relenting mud to black because so full
Of all the colours of lime, leaf and bough;

The electrix of the tree had clambered up my spine.

IV

Dare I wash my head again, with lightning
In the water, starlight
In the source? I went out to the stars,

Hedgehogs of light; there was no surcease,
Nor did I need one; like the thunder-source
The lightning in the black

Followed by creative shadow, the black
In which light forms and daylight breaks,
The lovely shadow kingdom, ablaze with shocking light.

THE PROPER HALO

In those glad days when I had hair,
I used to love to smarm it down with Brylcreem.
In those old days this was the definition of a boy:
A scowl, Brylcreem, and back pockets, admonished
To refrain from pomades at one's confirmation,

25

So that the Bishop would not get his hands oiled,
Greasy palms, laying them on. My uncle laughed at me,
And called me 'Horace!' with my flat-combed parting,
My head shining like a boot; though, as a Navy man,
He liked all that sort of thing himself,
Shaking a kind of Bay Rum out of a nozzled bottle
Labelled in Arabic that came from Egypt,
A brick-red Sphinx on yellow sand for scene,
Spidered with Arabic like uncombed hair. Retired,
He would send to London to the importers for it,
And I asked him what the spider-writing meant. He told me:
'If you want to be like Horace, employ our oil.'

When he died, he left me his personal things,
A wristwatch with a back pitted
From tropical sweat, studs and cufflinks
Glorified with tiny diamond-chips, a dressing-case
With hairbrushes useful to me then, his shaving-mirror;
I mourned him, but enjoyed using his things,
Conversing with his shade, taking both parts in the mirror,
Remembering how we talked, fascinated by this grown-up;
And I remembered catching the habit of hairgrease,
He dropping a little in my palm and showing me
How to rub it in with fingertips, 'You'll
Never lose it now, keep up the massage,'
Which wasn't true. Still, when he died
I did have hair, and liked the barber's shop.

A university friend staying with me
Translated the Arabic on the bottle,
Laughing. I said '*What* spirit?' and he said
'Definitely religious advertising; could your uncle
Read the Arabic?' I thought not, though he had
Many spoken phrases. 'Then he picked up "Horace"
From the vendor's gabble; it reads:
"Horus comes to greet you through this oil."'

I liked the barber's shop; the man
Stabs the pointed bottle at his palm;
My dark hair is cut and shaped and forests felled

Over my white-sheathed shoulders lie like toppled pines.
The oil shivers in the barber's palm,
He puts the plump bottle down, and that hand
Descends swooping on the other; they rub together
Like mating birds and as they fly to my head
I see they shine. His rough fingertips
Massage my scalp like the beating of a flock
Of doves; now it is my hair that shines
And stands up as though an ecclesiastical charge
Were passing through me; I laugh! 'You like
The scent of the oil, do you, Sir?' I nod,
Though I don't. It's the shine I love;
I shine with glory! and this is worth
The barber's shillings, many times. I shall feel
Of age as down the street I pass
In my shining pelt and glittering shako, my hair
Cut and shaped like my natural urges, properly, proudly,
In a halo of light and scent, godly contained.

THE PARTY IN THE WOODS

I

Each fly a little Isis,
A transformer, buzzing;
The trees worried by their wolf,
The wind. The spring of water,
An almost silent work, continuing
Under the threshold of sleep.
The little rivers of gnats.

II

The boy showed us a pleasant trick,
Taking his pennywhistle to the gnatswarm,
Which widened to the low notes like the outline
Of a Russian Doll that can never be

27

Overturned completely, and stretched up,
Whirling faster, like a skinny spindle
To the high scales, and with the music
The sunshine shone through every small
Illuminated body.

III

Sometimes we went the long way round,
By the ferry, just to get on the water
For ten minutes. A little spring
Had overflowed into the road
Making a sheet of mirror our tyres unzipped,
And this was as good to her as a festival,
Anything to do with water, falling water,
Flowing, anything, and the shower.

IV

We were not the first at the party in the wood.
The small dark woman in the great hat
Was sitting by the sheet on which the food was spread,
Waiting. The gnat-boy was one of her eight, the youngest.
Then there was the water-woman already mentioned
Who needed water to keep sane, and was beautifully so,
Who would sometimes walk in her street clothes straight into
    the shower;
Was, due to her use of water, the wife of her lover
(As he slept in their wooden house, he could hear always
The stream-work playing beneath his senses,
Sharpening them, sharpening them, for her).

V

After the picnic they made an expedition
To the old salt-cured casino on the railway-line,
Its salons half-drifted knee-deep up to the tables with sand,
Like crowds of players converted in their souls
To diamond dice, and standing on each others' faces
To follow the exhausted wheels, which was

Their spoil of the game, to be this fractured glass,
And their only speech the rubbing of this harsh talk
Which has so beautifully scoured the wooden house.

VI

Then there was a black man who dropped in when we were
    playing ghosts;
He put the sheet on in the dusk; and as it was too African
    a ghost,
Gibbering too much, my wife whisked it off,
But there was nothing underneath. No one saw him leave.
Everyone commented on the whiteness of my shirt,
From a distance they could not tell, they said,
Whether it was a radiation or a garment, and my approach
Was not frightening, with a hovering smile, my shirt
Falling like clean sleet from my pleasant laugh.

VII

She sung to us, the mother of eight,
Who has since stopped singing, like the demolition
Of old beloved places; her husband Luke had brought
His new wife, who might have passed for his daughter.
The two women tenderly embraced, the younger
Having brought wine and flowers, while he,
As if in affirmation of his new state,
Had grown his hair long, it was glossy
And black as eagle feathers, while she,
The mother of eight
Seemed thereafter to have no other state, no song.

VIII

Each fly a little Isis, a transformer
Singing its god-name over the picnic.
We fell to, and after, let them have it.
And the spring of water always singing.
I call my nearly invisible ghost to sing,
That which is black on black within, and strong,

29

Stronger than I am, sitting by the sheet's hem
Spread on the grass, held by the feast,
Helpless with love of the party, and of each one
Alive or dead who that day came to it.

THE FUNERAL
For N.

I

Clouds and mountains were invited, both the conscious
And the unconscious creatures. The trees
Like visible outpourings of the stream's music,
The urine of the animals in the dawn frost
Puffing like rifle-fire. The dark meat of the sun,
The bloody meat, the cremating sun.

II

Ninety-two percent of what we eat is from direct
Pollination by the bees, he tells me this
To cheer me and if true ninety-two percent
Of what he says with his mouth is said by bees. The first light
On leaves shines like apples hanging in the trees,
The whole forest a vast orchard, and all things
Are more than they seem, for they may fly away,
And disappear like Mother pausing on the threshold
Of the fields of light, which are like dew
Thick in the grassy meadows, for the light hangs
Dripping in the leaves, stands on the wind.

III

There is a Witness, I think, who has magnetic wings.
First it seemed to me at the funeral service with the terrible
Useless brass handles that would be saved screwed to
The veneer cardboard coffin which was much too small

That my emotions such as these swirled round my flesh
And some of them spurted from my eyes but ninety-two
    percent
Were beating in my back in a sensation like spread wings.
Since mine were sprouting I was able to see
The wings of others, such as my father's, standing next
    to me,
And his were ragged and tattered like those of an old moth
Close to drying up and drifting away, it seemed my duty
To merge my birth-wet wings with his, and this I did,
Entwining them in an embrace with him that he would never
    know,
And sure enough he, the widower, perked up,
And I felt tattered, but not dry, for back at the house
I sobbed my heart out in the little white-tiled loo,
And there was still a little angelic witness lodged in my spine
At the small of my back, in Jesus-robes, little calm watcher
In white, which I cannot explain, merely report.

IV

The other thing the funeral showed me, unpromising seance,
My Mother, subject of it, at the door ajar
On the field of light, looking back over her shoulder,
Smiling happiness and blessing me, the coherent veil
Of the radiant field humming with bees that lapped the
    water, and she bent
And washed her tired face away with dew and became a
    spirit.

PAPER DOOR

Her shadow glided across the paper;
I saw her go; the paper of the door,
The sliding paper door with
Painted horses running; her shadow

Passed over the cantering grass
Like a thundershower, and she was gone:

The freckled brass key tinkles in the slate lock,
The tumblers glide in bearings lined with mica.
We have shut the doors on that room, first the door
Of paper, then the stone and brass door. The sun
Roars with the door of itself open, the dawn-wind,
The herds that run down its thermal corridor
Scatter again, everywhere but in the empty room.

She returns round the edge of the paper
Bringing me tea and hot towels. In the limited patio
The buds of the tree are like nails hammered
Into a wooden ship, shining nails;
The little ship launches itself into the breeze. Even the tools
That men use become gods, and this
Is the reason for ceremony, the way
She returned, the hot towels, the tea,
Gods, gods; and she? Merely the woman
Returning, that was all, bringing the gods.

The room had been empty so long,
Until she returned round the edge of it,
Round the corner of the paper, a windless room,
A room without dawn. She takes
The papers out of the slate box, the paper headed
Deed, and another called Instrument, a third
Know By These Presents, and on these pages
Shadows have signed their names, the ancestors,

The ones that are free, leaving their papers,
Gliding through the sides of their deeds and books.
Brave ancestors, to die! the inks and pens
Become gods, if properly wrought, and the papers.
All will die, brave souls, and go among the herds,
Linger in the fragrance of hot tea like robes,
Cross the room and out at the paper edge, by these
    instruments;

No room can be closed or shuttered to these owners
Bringing their lights round the edges
Or borne on a lacquer tray by a young woman in a fragrance.

WARM STONE FOR N

I

Death as pure loss, or immutability.
A watch falling into the well,
Ticking a while in the cool spring, distributing

Its faint shock; or death
As a diamond-second in the year, set
Glittering cold in the anniversary,

The tiny diamond in her ear
Surviving the cremation?

II

Death suddenly appearing, like a spiderweb in the fog,
A piece of paper opening into a house, the snapshot
Through an open door, and at the table sitting still

Somebody; the house
With one room and no kitchen,
The house with the card door;

The disposable house.

III

I turn my back on the ascensions,
The unscreened smokestacks, I do not wish
To watch her ascending, the knots

Solving themselves, fading,
Climbing into the antechambers of rain.
Besides, her smoke should be white,

Blinding!

IV

And the colour of lost rain escaping!
And the photographs white
As the clothes are empty.

I open the prayer-book;
It is empty.

So, with her death,
I will baptise this small
Quartz; it shall stand for death

Like a glass room
Of which only a spirit knows the door,

Which only a spirit can enter
Turning and showing itself in the walls
Lined with warm mirror

Knowing its form in floor and ceiling,
Able to say 'I am here!'

V

It shall become a custom,
Warm room ringed to my finger,
Warm so long as I am warm,
Then left to my daughter

To keep warm, and bequeathed
To hers; warm stone
It will house multitudes.

MOTHER KHEB
(*For G.M.*)

I

The coffin, or dead-hole,
The soil-crib

Of Mother Kheb

Figured as the mine-mouthed hippo
With the spongy tread,

For she is the hole in the water
That ascends gasping,

She is an ark blowing
And the chariot that snorts.

And in the river of night coiling about her
There drill the seven stars,

Seven caves streaming with light.

II

Seven coffins blazing with the fire
Of their sleepers, and never consumed,

Save that they fade into first light,
And thus today is prepared for,

III

Since it is as great Caesar
Said of the natives,
That being descended
From the dark god Dis,

They compute their seasons
By counting the nights,

For them, today starts at sunset,

IV

For they reckon by startime
And date by darkness

By that star of evening marked out
Which is the morning star,

Star of the first time, the sign
Of yesterday and tomorrow, fulcrum Lucifer.

The bottomless graveyard of the night opens, full of
    awakening friends.

THE DRUMMING STARS
(*For G.M.*)

The game played in the dark. What is divine
Or inexplicable. A Peascod Wooing.
Find a pod with nine peas, put it on the lintel,

The first man who enters is the one; and this is
They say a hieroglyph of the nine gods,
The nine months of gestation,

The little orchestra of the watch, the nine months'
Watch, the percussion-group of the heart
Bent over its round measurer. Time passes. Burning the
    images

Of winter, rolling the fires down the hill
On St John's Day, the thunderstorms
Ramping like lions around

The circus of the horizon, the signs
Of the zodiac sliding by, the possible-to-be-born,
The different folk — the sun in turn

Is hanging their variable signs out.
A game played in the dark, a game played with stars
For nine months to the sound of a little drum;

A child soaked in darkness beats it,
The place where he beats it drums.

AN EGYPTIAN REQUIEM
For Wendy Taylor

I

Eat thy heart out, doing it
Amid the Hall of Clothes, the Hall
Of Transformations, the cataracts

Of forms, the lakes of mirrors,
The wardrobes of clouds, the
Sonata-in-three-movements Moon

Who dies, and her bones whiten,
And crumble into stars
And clouds, that quickly tense to dew,

Milliard of moon-fruit in orchards of grass
As if the Moon spread
Over all the earth, reflecting,

Poised to rise, the halls
And corridors of suits of light
Ready to rise in summits of cold,

Eat thy heart out
In thy transformations, doing it
Amid the hall of clothes,

Clapping thy empty hands
Clasped husks, like shells
Moon-white and bloodless, awaiting

By the flowing stream fresh garments,
And the Moon returns
Arraying itself in full, and you, knowing

The Lord was constituted here, out of the stars
Which are invisible by day, think
Of the wing of dew brushing all the grass

Shining powder of a wing, like moths,
Dab your hands in it, cool thy brow
In that which enters unto the Hall of Green

And drapes its clothes on every stem
Its mirror clothes, and great bending lens,
And steadies there, with a still gaze

As if on Judgment Day, when the damned avoid
The steady gaze of the saved; oh eat
Thy heart out waiting for that day

When all gazes should be steady
In the Hall of Transformations of he who assembles
All the lights in one. Beyond the Hall

Where you eat your heart, is a garden
Which still exists, though men deny it.
This is the starting-point

As when the Moon dies, and her bones whiten
And crumble into dust of stars, the nightside
Of phenomena where all transforms.

II

In sunlight on horseback
The hero races with his cruse of oil
Under the shades of oaks with his man's triacle,

Under the shades of oaks rending their gowns
That are their beauties, his clothes
Fluxing with their speed, bringing dew

For the Queen's garden, healing dew,
Like that which manifests at daybreak
And steadies there, as if it

Had always been, as in your waking head
Your sage dream steadies and regards
You like a mirror and a ready wing.

THE SISTER IN THE GLASS

The breathing-bells resounding of the hounds
Leaping in loose pack through the oak-tree shade,
The bumble-bee baby Om,

The red cheeks chafed to make you breathe
Your deepest, and speak, like air in bells;
The white-toothed claps of thunder that will not shake
   the rooks

Free from their fountaining trees as a loud cry
Or a handclap will; they wheel
Above the tree like little cinders,

Cinders that cry with the cold.
In the lightning of that clap the mirror
Photographs her frail form, and in the morning

I rub the clear glass marvelling
That her image is not arrayed there still.
It was a portrait of a micro-second,

A nano-second, a dwarf interval,
But a portrait to all my senses, for
The hair on me lifted as the cloud buckled

And the dark fell off her like the grave opening.
My fear opened doors in me, so that the garden
Sent zests into me through the window she had risen

To close, and the strains of her dress's folds exhaled
Several Flowers, then she turned, and the flash came
And there were two of her instantly,

One in the mirror, and herself. The one
You would call the real she; the other,
A person who had travelled on

Fast as light, but to see
That sister in the glass composed a moment
In which the thunder accelerated and climbed

The scales and was
The baby hum of a bumblebee and your cry
That went spinning off as I chafed your cheeks

To make you breathe, with the great cloud-dogs
Barking and sparking through their canopies
Fanged with lightning sheer

As a mirror struck in ivory with a sister
Who steps out in a flash and with a cry
Dauntless from the dog-tooth gate of thunder.

ASSEMBLY

I

Incessant movement everywhere
Initiates the assembly:
Small boats at dawn

Spread their sails
And sprint over the sea;
The night moth seeks haven

With the scented wind in its sleeves,
Flapping over the melon-gardens,
Librating with fleecy sleeves

Over the stiff pavilions of succulence;
Small boats ride
Their sails smelling of all the storms;

The great moths shed their caterpillars,
Pat their golden dust on your gentle hand.

II

The golden dust is smile-bestowing
And puts our sulky Princess-Abbess
Into a better mood;

I had felt rebuked
In the shadow of her back
As she turned abruptly

In the courtyard's gold-dusty sunlight.

III

It is well the parents
Have been packed off as if to bed,
To snooze in the cinema

41

Which they well understand,
They are sitting up with silvered heads
Watching the old, old films;

The veritable mirror-show
Would do nothing for them,
The comity of elders

Tucked up in the same wide bed
Of stories, sharing the same dream
Made of torn rays

Like moths burning,
Endlessly reforming.

IV

At the Abbey
The guests arrive
With their masks off,

The seniors and the elders
Unmasked;
And so the sea removes her face

Her elaborate face
Of the stone nostrils,
The whitened lip of coast,

The stone doorway
She is always passing through
Which rattles again;

The mountain
Doffs its white peaks;
The breezes untie their draperies;

And thus the magic of our Princess,
That certain magic the parents will not countenance,
Summons those

Who are already here
And who because of the greatness
Of their faces are not seen.

V

Do you frown at the show
Which creates magnetism?
Why, in all the mirrors the guests assemble.

This touch of breeze is the whole of the stars,
The sea is present as a ripple in the skin;
Do you frown at the mirror-show thus mounted?

Only the mirror-rubbing show creates
Magnetism sufficient to summon
Everything, she says,

Does the earth not put her turfy slippers
Off at our thresholds and appear within
Our clear mirrors polished by two girls together?

She asks, pouting, pointing her toe;
Are the most senior powers of all
Not female, she whispers, silkily?

THE GRAIN-SHAPED CAVE
(*Yoni*)

The barquentine *Mozart*
Gliding with its great palladian sails
Of light and shadow,

The earth herself, with her sailing clouds,
As if all her clothing shone,
The Goddess of the Shining Chamber;

Among the pillars of the docks
Like ranks of small iron castles
She hears the light, fleet steps

Chasing behind her
And cannot proceed,
Invites me to escort her.

There we learnt
To fill our blank in.
Each had a door flush into its side,

One could descend into the vaults
Into caves that are full of grain;
The stairs wind down

Light as the turbinals of gullskulls;
We brought our lamp to it,
It shone all over

Like a dungeon of mica,
Like a light in a well
That shivered its corridor,

Like a palace hung with shining fishscale,
Or close-fluttering with mothscale,
So when we entered this grain-shaped room

We uttered so great a sigh she had to go
And tell her father the whole story.

MUSK

I

A colourless afternoon
Full of grey clouds and rainwater.

A sound thinner than a clank
Many times repeated;
In the dark autumn morning
So many vessels
Enclosing sources of light.

The cousins limped home
With a broken grumbling sail
Along the boulevards of light,
And beached in the cove
Known as the Lobby of the Maid.

The great cave opens into the water;
It is the Maid herself.

II

How musky the room was when I opened the door!
And she would not speak at first.

That brave man, Mr Slaughter, was her father;
His trade was hacking the old houses to pieces;
The air of unsealed walls poured out of his sites.
He had opened secret rooms too,
Had unhatched their musks;
Once a hand behind an old fireplace
Kippered in the generations of smoke
Dropped like a batwing or a shed scar.

I took her out to see
The magnificent but indistinct
Appearance of the ships in the mist.
We walked cautiously, our hands sweating slightly.
We came to a place at the edge of Maid's Lobby
Where the land stops and there is only cliff-edge and mist.
It was a place which is both good and bad at once.
We returned through the weave of water and fire
Past the ships' sails pattering with their own cold rain.

Under the old oak she performed a trick requiring silence;
After it I was too stunned to think of anything
But congratulating us both, before we walked on.

MOTH ON GLOBE

I

Wings like fountains of felt gold;
Wings with geographies splashed across;
Felted gold soft as feathers; the earth flying
On its two great wings of tidal wave,

One wing bright with sunlight, the golden wing;
One silver with the moon;

The moon and the sun beating together
Their invisible feathers of magnetism
Within their light,

The infinite feathers folding, unfolding
The fathering wingbeats that bear up the worlds.

II

Breathing through her lumbar region
In triangular pose;
The wings of the white open shirt
Irradiating the face,
The throat full in its liberation,
The garments of summer.

III

The cocoon of a moth
Strung in its forceful gossamers,
Its aetherial bottle,

A genius in its bright lamp,
Its self-spun bottle,
That which is transformed
Into its soul from its two halves,
Clasped in its wings unclasping.

IV

A most
A moth
A moth on the lighted pane
Like a dry golden flame,
One wing bright silver,
One felted gold, powdery,

Powdery goddess,
Cat with wings,
Cloaked lioness

Divesting.

UNPASTEURIZED

The strange unpasteurized heights,
And that excellent suntanned all-copper
Waterworks sticker mechanism

With plastic ballcocks sucking at them
And snowflake zinc tanks sunk high
Into the arteries of a cloud-mountain
Of circulating ocean.

We empty the system and venture
With flaming torches into the mains,
Into the conduits maned with weed
That falls about our heads uncombed, which lead

Along strait routes to a booming cistern blown
In a domed cadenza of ancient bricks,

There are here tribes of black bats
Littering their crisp white skeletons

We lick our fretted lips
Free of their mermaid salts
And a few feet below the ceiling
A band of sparkling mineral crust;

As though one put his salt
Seed into the water, and seeded
Their reservoirs and clouds
So that all might become like him,

My unpasteurized father of the depths.

NATIONAL TRUST

The family portrait, and the earthly likeness
Serving scones. Sandwiches and suets
Were laid out on the side table.

There could have been blood in the gutters
From all that armour glittering in the hall,
But the armours were bloodless.

We stood munching at the trestle tables
Creating blood by our assimilations,
The Radio Three announcers announcing from their
    basements,

Their underground services running to time.
Each peach was like an immense sunset kiss.
The last rays waded in the little smoking streams.

All the trees had rounded their flanks like great homes,
Like great lungs smelling of grass, like magical robes,
Dioecious garments that are green with many tabs

And fruiting buttons, with seams all lined with flowers,
Garments grown, not made, the most humane of clothes.
The Radio Three announcers continue with

Their undying world spell, speaking to the world
From underneath the earth, ghosts of the cavern,
The ripe apple-tree like an immense sunset kiss,

The palms of the baby's hands soft and cool
As the segment of Satsuma orange I pass to her,
The May bough with its scent of semen, the sacred bough.

TRANSACTIONS

I

The waves break on the shore with a scent
Of briny cellars of sea-fungus shrouding
Drowned shiny forests. I have a white door
To my cellar which when I crack open
Is as though the house were a wave, stopped,
Overhanging, and in the still
Round cellar in that moment's time
The mushrooms manifested. I put them there.
A pulse of phosphorescence keeps the house up.

II

The little mushrooms are salt
And they smell of zest and venom.
I swim into the yesty air of the cellar
And see them stand like white circular messengers,
Helicopter-winged angels.
Stiff one-vertebra spine.

49

III

The pylons choiring in the wind
Marching like the X-rays of cathedrals
Along their zesty ozone spoor like the odour of mushrooms,
The earth spinning within its mother, the waters,
Around its father, the sun,
Within clear sight of its godmother,
The mob-capped, nectar-rayed moon.

IV

Whose white patched cap resembles a mushroom
Flying in its helicopter wings of magnetism
That raise the metal-sheeted tides
And crack them open scenting the sea-air with zest,
The pylons choiring,
Her silvery blouse flashing with electricity
Through its opening leaking her ozones
As the moonbeams scent the night-opening flowers,
My white shirt like an electric ghost
Specially laundered to enter this darkness
Under the cellar stairs where the white door stands open.

LIGHTS IN THE MIST

Lights in the mist branching across the water
Like fruit shining out of an orchard.
Then the mist clears, and the waves are disclosed
Stacked to the horizon, each with its poised sound,
Visible sound.

Her sleeping glances, her sleeping gloves,
Her body like some soft delectable debris
Awaiting collection. He breathed her odour in,
The carelessness of her relaxation overcame him
As no planned seduction could. He tastes the apple

She was eating when he began touching her.
The explosions of sea on the walls,
Random shell-bursts, traversing. Now she dreams

Of putting the final touches to the firstborn,
Knitting the baby's only garment with bone needles,
Engraving on the flesh the fingerprints like a colophon.

Dewy cobweb frozen like bone-of-lace; the orchard
Doing its one thing: creating leaves and fertilising flowers
And rounding fruit;

The water of the well twisting back into its brick socket.

Tasting alternately the cold earthy water, and the cool
Earthy fruits out of the apple-tree rooted in the wall.

The fenestral mists branching. The new veins branching.

CLOUDMOTHER
(*To D.P.*)

I

Several hot days,
The one after the other.

The standing cells of sunshine, lofty sunshine,
And in them blossom black thunderstorms.

Lathering clouds.
The wind tumbling in chunks.

The yachts tacking through the cells of gust,
Rigged like crescent moons, scudding.

The clouds the accumulated sails
Of the invisible wind-boats.

They throw their lightshadows,
Their visible loomings,

And they throw their windshadows,
The dark splashmarks of gust hurrying on.

The mountains in the distance
Steer the evening wind towards us.

The notes of bells
Blow towards us from the ravines of mountains

That halt the morning wind, and so
The long hot days, and the thunder

And the necessity for thunder, piling up
Like invisible pillars of the law: over the sea

Invisible and mere vapour, but over land
Which lifts the wind, it crystallises

Like silent moored navies awaiting orders.

II

A gap in the hedge which is a dry stream
Awaiting thunder. A footpath of dust to a wet valley.

My skin needed the wet meadow, I wanted to be
In that state of rest after thunder.

I considered the tree that gripped waters deeper than the dry
    stream
And the hedgerow in its roots, it

Considered me. The Cloudmother was glad
I noticed her, the invisible streamers

Pouring up from her boughs like
A reversed waterfall, patterning over the city.

I overheard a thought: 'The unmoved mover
That wishes to be moved,' then from her own

Accumulation of clouds her upper foliage fell
And shone, the Cloudmother hissing with the pleasure.

MOTHERS

The Mothers elect to keep their hair
Cropped quite short in close caps.
It is as they pitch their voices close,
Near voices without coiling timbres or
Disturbing undertones, just so their faces

Shall not be swung across with hair
Nor with unpredicted modulations the expression alter,
Nor a curtain sweep to give the child a glimpse
Of the other half of her feelings
Instead of the whole libration, the balanced face.
Another mother may well peer out of the left-hand side.

That would make Mother unreliable, or
Seductive, and stunt the growth. She
Must carry everywhere that certain voice,
And with her a certain structured cloud of fragrance,

A pleasant regulated scheme of odours
That are bedmaking, and kitchen,
Clean paint, and freshly-cut bread,

Like a balsamic mother-tree growing
Behind everything; that oak-avenue
Of Father's book-lined study, that
Alphabet-tree in the playroom tuck-box,
Joined at the Mother-trunk

Behind the appearance of everything,
A balsamic tree of odour everywhere,
A tree of flowering home. The Mother's hair
Is short and frank; and, recollect,
That maiden that she was had never learnt to swear
Or curse either before she made herself a Mother.

CUSTOMS
For G.M.

I

Flaming raisins snatched like souls
Out of the Keeper's bowl, the lowest sign,
The spark-holder, the snap-dragon of winter.

And the Doctor applies his bottle of light
To the fallen Slasher's mouth,
While going from house to house

As the Sun goeth forth out of the lowest sign

And our blackface is the dark
In which the sun was buried.

We dance in the lighted lanes
In the slant light, in blackface,

Blackened, bowing and bobbing
Blind man's Buff, all masked
Like the sun, who goeth forth,

Lifting his bowl of flame, full of green souls.

II

Now the giants stalk forth, in Summer
The giants on splay stilts,
We carry the green giants out;
With swishing boughs, we carry them.

A GHOST SONATA

I

He embarks on a phantasm for violin and another,
He who gathers his children under the beautiful tree
Lighted like an airliner at night, sintered lights
Sailing towards heaven, the tall and terraced tree
Pointed like an apparition on tiptoe,
The ghostly tree, containing them, each ghost
Tiptoe on a twig standing on needles
Upstretched because of the lanced feet or the aspiration,
With presents at its feet.

Oh, he that giveth gifts winneth the victory.

II

A phantom woman bathes at midday
To the sound of violins in the Fra Hollenbad,
The way to her home is through bathing in a lake pond or
    well.

At the touch of a button fresh water pours into an uncovered
    reservoir
Creating fresh doorways to the sound of overtures.

III

The Corn-Aunt roams about in the summer grain
You can see her invisible shape doing so, roams about in
    the rain;
I scatter a white shape of flour in the wind
To honour her and to feed the wind;

She wears the cap of invisibility
That is the mask of the shades,

Then at Harvest she doffs it,
She takes it off and is all those shining fruits,

Or the oat-field that we burned
And which is full of roasted cakes,

Or at winter, the tall tree tiptoed with lights.

My father gathers his children under this tree,
Plays to his children and the tree in violin,
Playing to the upsliding ladders of dewy soul,
Serenading the forest in wooden songs,
Nourishing our spirit and hers with ghosts and presents.

THE MAN FROM SELBORNE

In a toying manner
The cock pursued the hen.
His toy the hen.
The vast rains ceased.
The delicate weather now began.

I note the silent bird on the bough
Which, flying, chatters, passing through the air
Which rubs a tune from throat and feathers;

It is not the bird's the songster, but the air.

The vast massy buildings of that place,
The many waters round it.

The slender, dusky scarabaeus is the male worm;
The female is a lanthorn to him, and his toy.

The spring heads never freeze, the wagtails
Seek out the ever-flowing sources.

At midnight on Christmas Eve
To assemble beneath the thorn-tree
And listen for the bursting of the buds,
Their stealthy opening.

The sexes change garments and woo,
The goose-dancing, each is the other's toy,
Vying with each other
In politeness and gallantry, for ever.

CENSER MOUNTAIN

The Censer Mountain of balsam forests
That breathe and bend about us when the wind is right,
The mountain which utters its poem of wood,

Famed for its ingot-bright slugs condemned
To trailing wingless in sweet slime

Of which the ants partake
Joyfully;
And its fat moths that wing to our hinterlands

To hover at face height behind the glass
And stare at us with big gold buttons,
Or enter in like aerial puppies
To lap at our candles

While her whole ring grows rosy
And my warm snake
Flutters unbearably like a moth
Giving out a golden sensation.

The moths are gone, to their sensations,
Riding the altitudes of balsams
And sweet trails of airborne exudations;

Having sipped flame, we must sleep.

THE WILL OF NOVEMBER

The millionth leaf blowing along the path.
The sea white-headed, white-tailed.
Sky of wind-pounded ice.

Frozen bees shaken from their hives,
Rattling from the box like gravel.
The travelling shadows of the gravestones,

Oblong slots of mortal sundials
Among the puffs of young fog
Out of the brown wet grasses.

Oak like a telephone exchange
Full of birdcircuits talking,
Full of birds and no leaves,

Birds, not leaves.
Look higher: there the aeroplanes fly south, scoring
Skaters' tracks across the raftered ice.

SHE BELIEVES SHE HAS DIED

She believes she has died
Has become a spirit, naked as air,
So she steps out of her front door, nude as a peeled wand,
With peeled eyes, observing like a spirit.

There is an old tractor, a stiff fountain of rust;
She salutes as one invisible the squirrel, representative
Of the creatrix of the British Navy,
Who created the wooden ships by planting oaks,
Her presence passing does not hinder it, the rusty
Squirrel gnawing on a nut confirms her spirithood.

The elaborate bodies of death that people bequeath!
The house behind her, with its rustling wardrobes,
Those fleets of oak tall-masters, the oceans of clean water
Enough to float them which hasted through that body!

If you could see the perfume of the wood
Come rolling from its aisles! Older spirits might.
She passes through the meadows underneath the pylons
That flash and hum with their electricals, skeleton castles
Trapezing with ghosts, past the docks, the black
Spanish query of the great hook, the steel hulls
Booming with their riveting, like spirits
Battering to be released from flesh, or hymning,
On to the magnetism and glitter of the marshes, the little
    trees
With their backs bent laving their faces in the mud,

For she wishes to live again, and lave her body
In the mud, to make it heavy
Enough to live again; she straightens up
Her face glittering with it. The green lantern cabbages, the

Spotless mushrooms, are spirits compared to her now.

THE COLLEGE IN THE RESERVOIR

The body is the glass in which we see his spirit darkly.
Now the glass is broken he is invisible.

We catch his look in a rain-puddle,
In a mirror that is incompletely sheeted,

In the glasses reflecting as they are washed up.
I call him into this bowl of mercury,
Call him to answer;
To dismiss him I touch its surface with an iron rod
And his spirit can no longer float
On the agitated surfaces.
Poor ghost, tormented by the shaken surfaces.

If there were a still mind
Like that of a man meditating
Or a woman after her orgasm,
Then he could enter as a realisation,

Or into the mirror of the womb,
The sticky mirror, flypaper of spirits
Where they catch a-dying ninety years.
It will be ninety years
Before he becomes invisible again. That
Will teach him to linger!

Unless he catches cold
From the discontented germs of some plague;
These germs are like floating dust of shattered mirrors,
In the sandblast of a sneeze
They can scratch a reflecting surface so badly
That a person can become invisible from it and,
As we say, die, his glass frosted.

The glass hung for a little while in the body
Merely a room beyond a room in the inn,
Where we hide and seek a little while

Hang our mirror up for a little while.
Now he has gone beyond it, to the best of our knowledge.

His mother has gone on a little with him, a little touched.
She says, let's go and read the holy books on swings
So the swooping spirits can read them too,
Look, this is his swing, where I pushed him
High into the sky, and back again.
The spirits get pulled into the books about them,
Their reading wings bring dew hovering,
And twilight, into the playground.

The dew brushes the grass and catches there
Like a dove-grey wing covering all
That is composed of a million candleflames;
I fear for those trapped in the dew;

To travel the whole globe thirty-four times a year!
To forget proportion, racked in the blank clouds,
To round again in lenses brimming with light
And lose it again on the roundabout
Reeling from the taps and slipping into the guts,
Thus the whole town drinks the College of ghosts
Drowned in the reservoir and dissolved in shivering mirrors,
Torn mirrors of the web, whole mirror of the ocean.

THE MAN NAMED EAST

The dew, the healing dew, that appears
Like the dream, without warning, hovering on the blades;
The motions of his wings bring dew and light,

The man named East. The ghosts have lost
All sense of perspective
In the drinking-water, twisting and turning,

Shaped by too many vessels, and furrowed
By too many fearful vessels, for we
Drink the water of a drowned village

Of a drowned College from College Reservoir,
And across our drinking-water goes
A small yacht like a lighted kitchen,

A fishing-boat like a ruined cottage,
Dinghies like little violins
With squeaky rowlocks, with violin-voices,

With the devil's music written on the waters.
I stand by the small stream which contributes.
I kneel and dip my hand in, it insists

Into my palm with a slight pressure
Like a baby's hand, which is still
The elasticity of yards of water

Reaching down the hill
From the clouds on high; I crouch
With my hand in that baby's hand

Feeling the slight movement of its fingers,
The light clasp which is love,
The little bony stones rattle

And the cool flesh of glass sinews;
It babbles like a baby, I bend
My ear to the water and now I find

Underspeech I did not hear before;
With the forest like a vast moth
Settling its wings on the hill,

I dip my finger in my mouth and taste
Forests and air and the ice
Of the white rain-wing and its power-pinions.

62

A KINSMAN

I

Echoes, the cadavers of noises, bloated.
He has passed along the upper roads,
That is, as a risen spirit,
Not as an echo or similitude or reflection,
But concentrated, at focus, intensely bright.

II

The lightning confuses heaven and earth in its instant.
Those who die from it make vile concussed ghosts,
A virulent fulminate of heaven and earth.
He is not one of those whiteblack creatures
Like charred water.

III

I did not steal from him to harm him.
It was to affirm our ties, to manifest
And strengthen them. Such a joke
Is an excellent form of kinship, possibly
The only one; anyway
The only one we can endure, here below.

IV

Those terrible ghosts; one may sustain
A complete transformation, as the
Charcoal showers from blasted trees, white lightning
Transformed instantaneously into its opposite,
An albino struck by lightning in the womb.
We honour the chameleon changing from white to black
Like a dead African being reborn.

V

The grease that made him shine as usual, the cosmetics
We painted his cadaver with, they declared
His original richness, his potential radiance.
His earthly shine
Had touched me as with a hand, the palpable
And affable truth. He has an angel
That would light up the whole room
With a radiance the size of a pin's point
In which all my thefts would lie disclosed, forgiven
As among kinsmen sharing our goods and riches
Including my sly darkness and his radiance.

LESSON ON THE BANJO

Is sleep a mystery?
Or is it only a problem?
If it is a problem, it can be solved.
If a mystery, enacted only.
He plays the banjo record, to sleep.
Sometimes in his sleep he sings
To massed banjos.
At others, the anvil banjo-blows ringing,
He forges a head for himself there on an open anvil.

He sleeps among his shelves
Packed with the mushroom gills
Of each book shedding its black letter-spores
From its underneath black fertile sleeping-place
Out of the aware white author-mind that is round.
It is like forgetting everything he reads
Until night cometh,
Each fertile book shedding its letter-spores
In the reader's dark cellars, that shine in the dark;

Or the bookshelves in concertina-mood
Tune the banjos.
                              Opposite the library
Which he calls his home, across the estuary, there is a house
That from its windows and a wealthy high-fi every night
The sound of banjos sweeps out, a window which
Throws a great pane of gold light on the water,
As if, when it was time to sleep, a wheaty meadow,
Flooring the creek that separates them, floated up;

As if, when it was time to sleep,
Banjos manifested, an underwater garden manifested,
Devoted players aspiring humbly to the banjo manifested,
And the submarine dock floodlit where the guardian pod
Of nuclear submariners structured the night in banjo
As they wafted in. And whether

It was the loose strings of the water banjo-ships
Plying their shanties, or lighted mansions
And massed bands loosed from the shore gliding
In a flock of water-lights, sleep could not tell,
For moving down the Carrick Roads whole orchestras
Of banjos bowed and tucked, until he raised
His sleeping head into waking silence with one great window
Still lighted to the dawn. Recalling

The musical regatta he could say there was a presence
To whose honour the strung drums twanged,
Like a great mountain on fire
Or swooping hull of a star moored to earth
Upon whose slopes, miraculously unconsumed,
Were his head-smithy and his new-hammered face aglow
Circled round about by terraces
Of temples in the form of books with gilt-edged doors
Swinging open, free to all; they had the look
Of leather gates that trapped you
Among their twiggy votives until you hammered your
    headway out
Or like Orpheus on a banjo parlayed your path through
    the small black print.

65

IN AUTUMN EQUINOX

Black cat sitting in the scotch mist
A white sheen over her, every single hair
Piercing a water-bead

In a high magnetic autumn of electric sunsets,
My heart leaps in my chest like a cat
With a silver sheen on it jumping over a wall.

The sun, the enlightener, the whitener.
The snail has made his silk track over the berries.
Summits of water rise above

Cold summits of water.
The crowd, the myriad, the millions,
The region beyond the tomb,

This day on which the ghosts of those
Who have died during the year assemble
And prepare to follow the sun

Through the underworld as their leader
Into light, does not feel like death,
The white sheen over everything, that was mist.

On my walk over the hill I meet
A buddleia of the skyline
The blooms the same hue as the early evening sky,

So there are rooms in the bush
Where the sky seems to hang
And there are white butterflies at the flowers

Tugging and fluttering
As if the sky with its clouds
Had assembled like bloom, the bush hung

Thick with bunched sky and fluttering cloud;
While from time to time the silver underneaths
Of many leaves bend giving their sheen back

Like an electric shiver on this sky-tree;
And the long grass is full
Of big gunpowder-coloured birds who take off

With a detonation of wings, and to its thunderclap
A thunderhag rises out of the hills
Sliding sideways and gunpowder-hued,

Making our feet tingle
With its electrical presence, and in this field
Crouches an idle tractor visited by bees,

Great flower throbbing
With its metal scent, and a wasp
Nibbles at the grease ruched from two great pistons.

Now the mist returns:
All the spiderwebs — waterbeds! in the hedges
Every bush a contraption of sheen and waterbed.

At home in autumn
The dog's magnetic body
And its dynamite health abounding

Marking with its delighted pawprints the sensitive sheen,
Drives winter sickness from our blazing hearth.

SEASIDE CLINIC

The red tree climbs out of its marble grave,
The sycamore; I say be sick no more,
In the little white room by the seaside,
The white hairpin bend towards eternity

And back again. We are clothed white
Because we are to rise out of our bodies,
Out of the red, the dog-shit horn-of-plenty,
Into the white, and turn around,
And reinsert ourselves correctly,
With the doctor's blessings, and discharge again
Into the red world of roads.

The little hospital bed
Set exactly like a grave of steel and linen,
The great masks in white dresses, the nurses,
Their doubles in the dead black windows patrolling
The outer night-hospital where some are trapped
And bang up against the glass like souls
Who cannot get reinserted, jostling
The black mirror-backs, the great masks
In white small dresses of moths;

The sea in the daylit window like ranks
Of nurses all carrying white trays
Of gleaming instruments; or in the wind
That blows hard enough to pull the soul out,
The sea like a wet tree shaking out white blossom,

And harder still, kicking aside its skirts
Over its green chasms; did I see that
Or was I seeing it sleeping?
It is a way of seeking, the seaside clinic;
We are made dead to see the world of roads alive
Great masks full of the life that made them,
The business masks of chrome and petalled steel,
Plenteous among them. Now we know the only cure,

Seek no more, it is the magnetic sleep,
And bathing to music. I wash my sycamore scar
Perched on the sill of the tub,

With Luke, my husband, singing.

DIVA

I

The wet dog in the stream
Flaps and flutters
His shining water off

Like a star
A wet star
Under a firmament of stars, like dogs

Shaking themselves
Dark and dry.

II

In November
The myrtle that berries and flowers
At the same time, flowers

That star and stars that berry; the storms
Of fruit crush into that myrtle-bush;
Her blouse marked with myrtle-print, opening above

Into a matter beyond the gardens, her entire sweet pelt
So perceptive in these clothes
From the massage of air upon the throat,

Her collar widening like a torch-beam,
The open silk casting light deep into her throat,
Luminous angel in a ghost-shirt spotted with myrtles,

Singing among the myrtles with open throat.

III

With my staff up, stroking
The world within gently with her silk
To the sound of her recorded song in which

Death gives her the power to fly;
To the sound of the record,
The whirling post-mortem voice,

I visited the bone-lands,
The seeming mansions of sepulchral chalk
(Thank god, against the white, naturally

Ghosts remain unseen)
Only myrtles there,
Both flower and fruit;

Thus she attended me, invisibly, in her blouse,
The vinyl voice circling the post.

IV

The spark-gap at the thorn's tip,
Where the water-drop flashes. Which
Came first, proposition,

Or apparition? They came serpenting,
Alternating in the echo-sounding clothes,
Visible blooms of heat, the colour of chanting,

Collar of myrtles, the sleeves, the skirts,
Direct eloquence sparking,
Eloquence with heart, with odour of silk,

The sweet smells of the chanting person
In the myrtle-garden, in the rain,
Who ran back into the thorny ruined church without
    warning,

Stars flying out of her hands,
Running down her sleeves, into her song,
Springing from her lips and throat, flashing.

WHITSUNWIND

The aerodynamics of the hold of the house,
Our wooden, cello-voiced ship,
The hull of the house, its grip on the wind,

The sheets and rigging of the beds
As they dream their noisy voyages,
Its heeling in the seaweather,

Marvel of nailed timber,
My carriage which thunders:
The dead trees of it resurrect and

Howl through their corridors
Like huge fires passing by on either hand.
I draw a tumbler of foaming weir, let there be

Weir foaming out of all the taps, I run
From tap to tap to augment the sound,
And all the lights on too, trees of lightning

With fruits of thunder,
Wagner on the recorder;
There are ghosts enough to rattle all the bolts

Like nuts in their wooden cases, and the nails
Bow silkily their grains; such bottles
Of stouted fire, and the charged air,

And the sea wind rushing with its manes
To leap the mansards packed with light
And groaning like string orchestras.

Now, the calm of Whitsunday. The waxy seed
Of grasses that shines over the field
Of light laid down like mother o'pearl,

And the sea still rocks, and in the ears
Water-radios in stereo sealed in a cave,
Two coiled shells like cockles locked in chalk,

Small twin blowholes taking the air's full fetch;
The sea quietly puffs tons
Of white sound at them in Whitsun.

RUSTY BREATH
(*For J.H. Barclay*)

We are polished by our travelling, as the train sways
We are fencers of thinbright iron that continues distances,
Prolongs. We breathe the rail
By that express vaporised, it becomes
Iron of blood, by the blacksmith of the chest
Beaten behind the ribs and grinning beard.

Like a restless skeleton shunting bones
From foot to head and back again, our clanging train
Pauses by a freightyard, the restless, dead
Sonorous things. Now off again
Under our wheels the hiss
Of steel on steel, our journey
Stretches excited like thin blades endlessly
Drawn from scabbards, we speed
Like important messages along taut wires that sing, the
    stations
Smell of polished iron and bundled newsprint, dampened
With our thunderous sprays along
Iron sheer with centuries of railway.

Our travellers' blood is up, like freightyards flurries,
Because of off hot miles the smells of excited iron,
Railway iron, like the long journeys of the blood,
Blood answering the iron, a travelling steel, polished
And polished again by the timetable, and the round iron trucks

Spin on their rustless veins. The journey is too long,
The iron too strong
That smells like steel on the alighting schoolboy's breath,
Like iron wine breathed as he embraces hard his mummy.
My blood needs alcohol, I spill some metal
As fee and fare, and carriages clash like coinages.

SOFT HANDLING

Lanterns made of shells burning crab-oil,
Crab-shell lights, luminous carapace,
Shining spiders. His snowy hair

Was a ghostly sign to follow
Across the darkened beaches,
He with his whisky-bottle,

Little square powerhouse.
The headlights in the rockpools
Were like folk wandering between the stones

With torches lit. The ocean became aware of him
As he of it. At midday when he returned
It played its folding searchlights

Over him from its concave reflectors, its convex
Reflectors, the ocean with its shining fronts.
Where is there more nakedness? The pandar,

The sun, marking its pathway across the waters,
The moon, pandar, printing its white footpaths,
Whiter than Jesus' tread, sacred office, and there is

No better stone than the stone of this pathway
Across the beam-haunted beaches to her beachhouse.
The soft handling over and over, hour

Upon hour. Is God himself
More naked? Like a moth
Fluttering among her sheets dry and chalky,

The skin which flutters unbearably
Like a moth scorched
Charring the hot dome of the electric bulb, among

All her dressing-table weaponry, her dangerous
Symbols, a sheer silk shirt, the design
Of a river of sparrows upon grey satin, like

A great serpent of satin lolling in her sheets,
With she the mesmerist of the world, striking us still,
Our souls fled in perfume and mingling elsewhere;

This river of souls must end among the stars
Like all rivers, in their clouds. After
Drinking the whole powerhouse

It was hot Weetabix for breakfast
With powdered coffee on it, which she took,
Great serpent of satin in her sheets, like a river

From the stars, and when the light was off
In the headlights from the road the bed
Shone like the moon. The symbol, the sheer

Sparrow-shirt, donned, assembled her body
Into a vehicle that expressed
A certain flashing, serpentine path across its waves,

Becoming aware of me because of its fronts,
Its folding reflectors, the buffets of that light.

FETISH

I

There was this man went to the prostitute
For a special thing. Put on these gloves,

He told her, long creamy kid-gloves, unfolding them
From a wallet, nearly to the elbow. They are just

My size, she said, surprised. All the better
To love you, he said, sit here, be still and please

Just feel and say nothing. What are you going
To do to me? Just this: began stroking

Her gloves, stroking, down the outside
Forearm, up the inside, stroking, stroking

Gloves. That's all, he said, give me back my gloves,
And thank you. Something for the maid, she told him.

II

The clothes stroke themselves,
Creating their electricities,

That lighten in the sleeves,
Mutter in the skirts,

Swirl from these fixed buttons in a too-great touch.
Gloves may well be enough.

The openings in the stuffs create electrix
And focus it in alternating plates,

Batteries of warm-cold, warm-cold, and the skin wakes
In feelings and blind thoughts from shapes of clothes

Whether they gather or whither they flow,
Their pondering, the pull, their libration

Of lapel, gradient of cleavage, the wading wind
Melting the skin

In deltas at the neck where the pearl-string bounces,
In estuaries and marshes vivid with wings,

Springy with curled grass in the unseen rays
Of the invisible skin; where it shows

It blinds us, we turn away, the force
Of nakedness shines like a sun within

On fabrics that spring
With pattering canopies of leaves,

Rivers ever-sliding, and fruits
Taking their form in clothes. He said

This goaty leather of the dead, I stroke it
Into the here and now. All right,

She said, but normal costs extra.

THE BROTHEL IN FAIRYLAND
(*Madame Twoswords — Goddess-patroness of brothels*)

The courtesan with a taper guides
A young man to her mosquito-net.

There is a river-party in full swing
With hired geisha, and three courtesans
Dance their winding dance on the
Landing-stage of a teahouse. It is called

A teahouse where we drink the girls
And meditate on the tea, the women
Dressed like peony-gardens fill the fairyland
Of painted screens and doors, their shadows
Lie solid on the layers of mosquito-net

Where a woman holds up a stone saké-dish
With cherry-blossoms in it and beckons to a client
Unseen behind the mosquito-net, the stone steps
Shine with the little hovering lamps,

And a lighted-up pleasure-boat like a wedding-cake
Iced with light, a 'fairy-boat',
Does its winding dance
Like a torchlit procession down the guts of the river;
It passes on the current swiftly; we glimpse
On the deck a woman holding up a bamboo cage
Of fireflies and pointing at them.

In Japanese, 'fairyland', in English, 'brothel'.

The fairyland is full of candlelight, perfumes, and electrical
    skins,
You can feel them as they pass by on their currents swiftly
Entering your skin and leaving it, gliding by
In their visible skirts, touching you
With their invisible clothes, their electrical dress
Such as a forest also makes, or a wooden scow
Blazing with candles, or a swift-flowing river makes;

With a screen by the enclosure announcing business
And a shaped electrical neon picture of Madame Twoswords,
Lightning in a peony gown. Many holy ghosts

Crowd round her to see the outcome of that fight.

MOTHERS AND CHILD

I

The soft modelling for hours,
The soft handling.
Undressing, she forgets to say her prayers.

The town of wives, promenading,
Staring among the lighted beauty-shops
Which are shadows of the beauty that is above,

That is too bright to look at
Except in the shadowing of lipstick and powder,
Painting with colour, camera obscura,

This in the town of the two electricities,
The powerhouse, lighting the shops,
The wives, stiff in their orgasms

With fingers stretched like starfish
And eyes going like electric bulbs,
Witch-hair cracking the taut white pillow;

And the stiff filamentous reach of the powerstation
Incandescent also in its circuits
Like some miraculous gestating glow-worm

Or silk-spinner of tungsten
That shines with that power,
The elastic of magnetism,

For whirl wheel within wheel
It comes spitting
Into the lamps, over the sheets

Of the great metropolis of rooms
And the lighted villages of wives
With the lover wanting the skin off

Wanting the electricity in essence,
The stripped wires,
Electricity with its rubber off,

Electricity more naked than last time;
He strokes for hours
Mowing the magnetism,

The sheets crackling,
The soft handling over and over,
And gradually the first skins loosen;

And the wives observe this recreation
As the mother her rounding belly
And wishes her child to be naked of it

Herself now willing her own birth
As the fish skips out of the wave
To be nude of the water

Water that peels off water as it marches
Nakedness off salt nakedness,
So that, undressing, she forgets to say her prayers,

As water forgets, and reflects
The beauty above her.

II

Or does she beam beauty up
To be bounced off the ceiling
Or off the man above her,

Transforming her beauty
Into his (and he needs it);
Her fighting-gear

A silk shirt,
Excellent accumulator of electricities,
Admirable rubbing battery of orgasms,

79

Or, as they say, Static,
For time stands still.
Such heroes as there might be

Awake when they touch her skin,
With a silent shout of recognition,
Skin which flutters unbearably

When they touch it sufficiently,
Like a moth beating in the light of the sheets,
The moth whose wings are flaming

Without being consumed;
And the wellspring where the more it is drawn
The more it flows;

While the wife as mother of herself opens
And draws herself off
That which steps out

Over the sill, the berth, the landing-place.

THE PALE BROWS OF LIGHTNING

The small pale-browed horse waiting.
The three golden instruments:
Trombone, tuba, trumpet.
The moon like a round sail.
Great stone barrels of sea-sand:
The kind that blows about
Sparkling, becoming wind-smooth,
Used to fill hour-glasses.

How many times in the hour
Does the lightning strike
Fusing elf-arrows in the dunes,
Attacking the springs,

80

The little brooks leaping in steam?
In this dune silence
The forces from which the lightning springs
Held apart in the silence of nature
On which the three golden instruments
Set forth out of their transistor
Rising like birds towards the thunder
Which bends down, listening, as he
Bends and gauges her readiness
By the excitement of her lips,
The sitz in her kiss, while
The trombones blow, waiting for lightning.
In the dunes, are they safe?
The infinite resources of shame,
The lightning that flows from it;
Somewhere in its career
Every cloud is bound to develop
Into a flash of lightning;
It is its evolution
To become a torrent
Of electricity
Like a mighty reversed tree
Tossing great stones up
And splitting them in mid-air,
Great dark flints full of flashes
And infinite resources,
Among the pale-browed dunes
Of cool sand, and the transistor
Full of small gravel that blows
Golden tubas, his dark brow
Estimating her charge, by her silence;

And lightning opens its shutter but an instant,
When it catches you burn like a candle,
What is that lambent shadow fluttering into the woods
In its own blue light that illumines primrose
The ripped tree's flesh?

It is time, but will he recall lightning
Or the clouds of shame merely, that gather?

It is her discipline not to permit them
And with a differing kiss she clarifies him
Being full of his lightning and his sitz.
The bolt struck the old thorn-bush, in the corner
Of the field, but for its afterflash
It blossomed without flowers, sending out
Its sweet perfume that clarified shame,
And the small horse who had galloped away
From the whirling pillar of snap
And the pale ghost of steam of an afterflash
Came back to breathe the may-scent of the burst grain;

And her perfume articulates,
She points and speaks as the night descends
And they walk out of the dunes towards the beach
Where the ships at evening compose their light
In points, like stars in granite
Lightning-struck; and each ship
Compassed about its great wheel,
The mandala you steer by,
Its ten mahogany spokes, its nub of brass,
Great round tree pointing your route
Between the water-spouts and the lightning-strikes;

Ship at night compounded of points of light
Like a comet made of ice
Steering among the crackling spheres
With its light-year transparent sail plunging.

LIKE A ROCK

Rain marks cold coins in the water.
When she wears a shirt, a blouse,
It is as if she were dressed in water;

The whole river turns with her
And crinkles with her breathbeat.
I have seen a rock in the

Fast stream dressed
In a beautiful shawl of water
Hunched round the shoulders and

Open in front; I have seen
A smooth rock standing
In a waterfall, dressed

In a never-ending weave
Of water-trails down the stream,
A twisted glass shirt like flame,

Like a personage
On whose head light beats
And refines him utterly down to the tail

During many centuries. When
She wears a shirt, or blouse,
This is saying: thus

I glisten, and ripple so,
Under my skin and in my secrets,
And I am dressed like this for you to

Prepare your entry and stand
As a rock does in flowing water.

IN NORWICH MUSEUM

The rock-tree underground
Moving its boughs slowly,
The sky-blue flintfruits

Rising in the soil
Gradually like sealed firmaments,

Knapped open they show
Blue and cloudy white;
Like sky-blue apples falling upwards

Very slowly. The hollow blue-black
Underground tree of the mine,
The thick orchards of the mines
Berried with flints, and these blue fruits

Are full of stars, their darkness
When struck is full of stars, a sneeze

Of stars, like the grindstone
At the cottage door sparking in the twilight.

The mining tools in the flint mines
Were flint axes, fruits
Cut down with themselves, as though
I used wooden axes to cut down elms,
Or inspired by cider combed my boughs of apples.

The shafts were excavated with antler picks,
Thirty feet down through chalk and sand,
For the best flint called Floorstone;

The hairy matriarchs
Dug by the light of pith wicks
Floating in animal fat in chalk lamps,
Like their own bright eyes
Floating in their chalky skulls;
I inspect three skulls of matriarchs now,
In glass cases smeared with fingerprints;

The sparks of their picks groping the walls,
The rock-tree's underground shifting
Its tunnelled boughs slowly, matriarchs
Crawling inside the hollow boughs creaking

Their stone leaves full of fruit, whose falls sometimes
Crushed them as in flint-glass mills.

TOO OLD FOR BONES

With a nasty irate cough
The slater is kersing
Among his hammer-taps

The gable-end with slate
Hanging scales like the keeper
Constructing a museum fish.

His ladder rises from the clay-place,
The nettly churchyard
Where the grave people reign,

The place of concealment.
He hangs slate and knocks nails
Into the house of the little cakes

Which celebrates the return of the dead
With small moons made of wheat,
Like lunar images of the reflecting field,

The infinite mirror
Of wheat whose tops are tidal
And whose roots are grave.

The churchyard dog,
The kenner in his kennel,
Is cold and old, kept

In a hutch with a cross,
Too old for bones.
The birth-cake whelks again,

Which is to wax moon-round
For the child,
The whole year baked into a moon

In the parson's house of the dead,
Or spiritual living,
Where the Revenant visits her mortal love

Not as a slinky sprite or will o' the wisp
But as a cloud of hailstones
With a striking albedo

Rushing over the sea,
With its million white globes
Dashing us white,

Great castle of ice
Blowing into faceted cobbles
Seen static on all the radio sets.

Now stars in the sky
Stand as thick as dew on the pane
As thick as the hail

Rolling down the kerser's slates,
Dew on the black angel's wing
And the night sea breaking

White over black rocks.
It is a whiteness of spring
The hail like the solid memory of mayblossom,

The bones of blossom. In the clay-place
One startling monument
Is a giant labourer

Standing amazed with his feet
Trampling the vat, astonished
At the resurrection.

On his sleeve crouches
A bass-clef snail;
Moss in the roof-gutter

Padded like a green-gold mouse
Twitches whiskers to the
New smell in the air

Of stone as the Moon rises.
Now everything tastes and smells
Old as the cold moon and the new slate roof.

THE INVISIBLE MAN & CO.

Tie a mirror,
Casement of deep indeterminacy,
To the springy branches
To snare the beautiful bird
That homes on its flashing beam,
Is amazed by its silent portrait,
Sings to it, to cause it to sing,

And as it sings
Pure pearls
Float out of its beak,
Rattle to the ground
Like an unstrung necklace,
The singing tree of bird and mirror
Showers pearls that gravel the path
Like graupel hail.

By the captivation of the bird
The Saviour
Is manifesting, or has manifested,
The Invisible Saviour who was turned
With blind eyes into the mirror-land,
He is being drawn
Like pearls out of the mirror.

The Invisible Man is blind
For the reason that you cannot
Take pictures with a glass camera,
But he has been transformed
By the self-capture of the jewellery-bird

Into a wonderful pearler's shop of mirrors
In which His Sister sings and serves,

And we see further that
Either He or She
Has become the Moonshop,
Stone emporium that rises over the roofs,
That unfolds pleated mooncloth whole
Out of its one full round shopwindow,

Because the bird sings to the mirror
And slowly the Invisible Man returns
Looking around him declaring
'I can see!' for he had thought
He walked in blackness, while all the time
We noted his perfect transparency
And how the articles he used,
Fingered by him in total night,
Perched or hovered like the blessed birds.

The moon sails like a round boat
That is all porthole, and the pearls
Patter piercingly. Now the Sister

Sells a heart-shaped bride-pillow broidered
And empatterned with pearls in staves
Scoring a bridal march for organ,

For tucking under the buttocks to tilt
Exactly the grain-shaped cave, the chamber
Of pleasure (insufficient term) as one adjusts

The tilt of a telescope so that the images above
May slide without check down its sweet straight barrel.

88

WORD

I

Women offer mastery
Of night. The quiet
Recording of beetles in the wood
Like writers in libraries.
A child's little hand
Cool as mushrooms. A black
Beard like a curse just uttered
Congealing about his lips.
He strikes her, the night
Explodes in needle sparks.

II

The fresh smell comes off
The lawn before the rain,
Prefiguring the rain,
The grass answers with perfume
To the tension of the clouds.
I turn on full the mains
Cold water and rinse the memory
Of the blow off my hands again and again.

III

The bees, drinking,
Settle on the wet mud. The swan
Scales the stepped air
With buffeting wings,
The booming geese
Voyage on in their long clothes.
I step with my whole leg
In deep mud, its perfume
Unfolds, the wet
Groans like the vaults of night
To the flight of sheer geese.
The child with her hand

Cool as mushrooms
Grips mine, with her
Wholesome skinsmell, of what

IV

Is she made?
The evening shadows
Grow like a beard from the trees,
A tangled beard. It needs
A grown woman to give mastery
Of the night. The beetles
Devour with the sound of nibs
Forming their oval tomes
(The scroll in the vase of skin),
Beneath the carapace
The potter's wheel with its chafing sound,
In glossy carapace,
Whose freshness is its tome,
Its theme. By no means
Is this blackness a curse
To the mastery of a grown woman.

V

Who teaches the little death
With its needle constellations, its
Relaxations into new metals
And ripening substances of night, the memory
Rinsed clean, the tomb
Sealed only as a potent book
Not to be split before time,
Not before the blast of death
Has ceased exploding
Its too-great mudsmells;
The soul stands in a tall
Bell that is ringing still, escapes
In carillons of night-smells
Pleasing to God whose skin

VI

Is everywhere and never dies. Consider
The little deaths like tottering steps,
The mastery of walking offered, in death,
Of reading, and of parable,
Offered by the grown woman, mastery

VII

Of the great skin-bound book
Wrenched open, pouring forth
Its smells of glue and ink,
The echoes of its tales
Sparkling like mushrooms
Splitting their veils
In the wet fields cool as the hands
Of children, the words
Walking through the dew or drinking it,
The words in white wings
Scaling the broad stairs of the dusk,
The words spreading in round echoes,
The snow-capped geese burst
Out of the bone-bound book entitled
White in yolk and feathers.

THE WHEEL

I

The moon's full beam of solid silver,
Its shaft of grey ice travelling onwards,
The steering wheel of the moon, full.

Water, in its cosmic form of ice.
Cars made of the ices of metals
With wheels to steer the crystals.

The skull is made of calcite crystals
And steered by its wide wondering eyes
And its basic eternal smile.

II

The crystal as the moment of patterned clarity,
Of understanding, unveiled, then veiled again,
As the snowfall, wheel upon wheel;

The animals and the stones, trees, metals, jewels
Wheeling round the magician in his zodiac,
And the sun as gold foundation, conductor's dais.

III

In the moon's light, the oceans steer,
The rivers wax, and dim, their streams,
The weir hums high, or runs silent

Deep and strong through wheel-spun sluices,
And he listens to the stars like wheels,
Listens through radio-wheels to the stars,

Through radio-telescopes, that are dish antennae
As are your blue-lidded eyes that star-gaze
On wheeling music that shakes like spiderweb

Everlastingly our bones to crystal dust.
And the name of the thing, the wheel
By which I steer it, is fastened

To the whole creaking ship
That is nailed to the pole-star
By the wheel of navigation

That I grasp and turn, and the universe
In me turns, the sails of stars
Flapping and dripping radiance,

The pricked sheets of constellations
Through which we see total light,
My ship being

On a new course.

III

Alchemy; to turn something which appears
Worthless into a matter of virtue,
Into a crystal like a wheel you can turn.

With an effort I twist the whole mass into a new course
Which it follows smoothly, the ship
That was a forest stripped from its hill,

A small forest diverted from its root-course,
Its seeding and reseeding, to the graven sea-roads,
The creaking woodland driven by the wheel, the wind,

By flowering sails and urgent constellations.

WOODEN WHEAT

As the ear of the wheat, the cone
Of the pine. A bunch
Of wooden ears, the wooden
Honeycomb dripping with balsam
Tasting of cough-drops,
Ligneous cog; and aphids

In swarms like a tremendous crop
Of green apricots with legs, big
Glass bums of clear emerald syrups.

Over there a modern hotel
Among the terraced needles,
Like a luxury liner washed up in wooden tides,

The green-shadowed fish of air
Vaulting through their rollers, feathered fishes
With ample wings, and everywhere
A pine cone, like wooden roses
Perfumed with cough-balsam;

Or a cabinet of ears that prick up in the sunshine,
Or a comb of wooden eyelids curiously jointed
Opening upon honey; a cabinet

Of wooden eyelids most marvellously jointed
And overlapping like an Islamic masterpiece
That falls open with a click, spreading;
A cabinet of a hundred lids that all at once
Unlock. It is full
Of yellow dusts and sherberts, each grain
Elaborately carved, carving within carving.

Unripe it is green and like a spindle
Of green fingernails tipped with red,

Of green fingernails that begin to tap and click
As falling off the bough this gift rolls
Into the patch of hot sun and starts to stretch.

Many remain fastened to the tree
Like dark lanterns engraved
All over with sealed eyes.

THE COMFORTER

I

The spectrum of all honeys, the sweet rainbow:
White clover; green honey
Of sycamore and limetree; acacia of pale gold

And brilliant sun-honey of dandelion; almost-black
Gathered from chestnut and buckwheat;
The fetid honey of the laurel

Of privet and ragwort too, though to the bees
It is excellent, they help themselves freely;
And the thyme and rosemary are ever-thick with bees.

II

Fume of their last feast before winter;
Bees, butterflies and the big old wasps
All feast in wintery weather

On the pale-green and circular ivy flowers,
The peaceable feast of the carnivores,
The carrions and the vegetarians all together;

The wasps, the bees and the flies,
And the hover-flies, imitation meateaters,
Wrapped in the tiger-hides of wasps;

And the beetles of the interiors
That pace at beetle-tempo the powdery pistils,
The yellow-green beads in circular dishes,

They peaceably feast on together, play you
A fume of organ-note as you pass by.

III

He was very relaxed, and his senses, like fibres
Had expanded to every corner of his airy room.
A single fly entered. It was a little torso of fluid

It was a little water-bell carved with a mask.
It had squeezed the grasses to fill itself,
It had distilled in the sunshine many dungs

And sang such a luminous note,
A green light in it.

IV

Travelling the line of its buzz
Which vaults in spiral around its flight-path
And is a corridor of sound

Vibrating like a cloister,
The fly hurries and hums
Like a monk at his chant

At his work in the crypts of distillation
Sealing bottles of fly-spirit, like a Benedictine,
Flasks catapulting more swarms of hooded hurriers.

V

An E, he thought, the hummer of an E,
And he hummed one, with all the flies of the day
Humming their E and sitting down

To their feasts of seeds and across the spectrum of honeys
And to their darker refreshment, the whole day
A banquet and never-ceasing prayer.

The room grew full of tall grasses, shadows of late summer,
Vibrating as rushes vibrate. In his dark mood
It was his elbows bent and his head thrust into its dungs
   like a fly;

Now that mood was beautiful, the Creator flew.

SERPENT OF THE MONTH CLUB
(*For G.M.*)

It is like an eel crawling the mud at speed
And the back water of the abyss,
A man fishing, in Lorn, saw it,

Passing from morn to sunset, passing,
That was a long eel, and the completion
Of its circle pierces the deep.

And the giant of a month old;
The lunar month is a pinioned giant
Held by rachets of seconds, to which

It is gigantic, seen by the wheeling minute;
Each cog floats by like a mote of pulses
In the great eye of the year.

But we need the second's flying eye
To enter by, its eye and understanding, for the way
To the eternal is by means of

Gigantic circles of time, spiralling towers
That comprehend the great circle that describes the small
And the minute the great, astronomical towers

Studded with stars and packed with centuries
In cockling stairs; I pass
From the opening of the second to the

97

Open eye of the year, permitted? peering
Out of the giant's eye and watching the dwarves dance
On summer greens among the summer giants

Who dance upon their timber poles of foliage;
And winter time is an almost-immovable
Hoarfrost giant — the cyclops of the Sun

The three-headed Moon, Oh
Holy race, to whom such deities as these
Are born in their gardens;

That is, a circle of time, or attention,
Repeated rings, the onion,
The year that flies and undulates

As a serpent does, or the Lorn eel,
Gliding through the great mud,
Forests asleep under its gritty winter lid.

LIGHT BLACK REDSKIN

He had a camera photograph
The interior of a camera,
That most sacred place,

The arcanum into which the pictures flooded
And froze in silver on the temple back wall —
That was, he believed, the gestating darkness

Into which souls entered, holy analogue.
He desired one eye removed
So that by shutting his good one

He could contemplate the blackness beyond blackness
That was the empty socket, and conceive.
Men were blinded by sight, and the camera

98

Had become a trader's stall
A silver source
Flooding the world with blinding images;

While truly it is a little altar
Sacrificing film to shutter-mechanisms
That with their incredible celerity,

Their nano-seconds, their dwarf-moments,
Could come just a little closer to no-time
And let just enough God in sometimes

Frozen to the wall
With stilled wings and staring silver eyes.
The Red Indian photographer said this, and more.

Such as let that blackness in, grasp
That emptiness within the box,
The unstained glass! and thus

His photographs got small as soot,
Then larger and larger, he snapped
Water of the Challenger Abyss

With weighted cameras full of water
So it was the deep you saw, and not the sea,
The emptiness of a great black plate

Exposed for weeks and clear as a window from the deep,
And he photographed the blazing night sky,
Cut all the bright stars out and pasted

The black bits together. He photographed
The blackness of the moon as it rose
In the sun's centre and was in the radiance of the dawn

Perfect negative, all stain, and a skinny model
Swallowed a camera shut into a pill, set
To snap its shutter in her bowels,

But there was a beautiful golden light down there,
The thin girl was translucent, as the thinning womb
Is to the unborn child, even the fattest

Were not opaque — so he must conclude
There is no arcanum without light,
Snipping a luminous sting-ray out of the suave abyss.

So he swept his floor and took up images again
Photographing his ancestors in the bright sun
With staring eyes

Pounding the reservation earth in their rain-fringed ghost-
    shirts.

YOGA CRONIES

I

The vapours rising from the seas,
Where water and light marry,
And matter receives the stars' signatures,

Every atom receives the whole;
This the yoginis know,
The cronies, associates of the Crone,

Breathing with the salt sounds of the caves
And the tidal cattle lowing to and fro,
Squat-legged on the grass of morning,

Breathing with the sounds of serpents,
Is-is, Is-is,
Among the dew's harmonious exhalations,

Breathing into the sunlight as the dew breathes,
Breathing, which contains the essence of all,
Rounding the whole chest with two inner wings,

Creating the fresh elixir that has been contrived
By the soul's prostration on the outbreath.

II

She saw one of the paths grow brighter
As darkness fell. Gold had in the past been found
Mingled in the sand-dunes, but when the wind

Raised by correct breathing had blown all night,
And when the sand shifted,
It left a one whole great ridge of gold

On which the cronies sat together celebrating
And giving thanks unto their mistress
Who taught them breathing like toothless serpents

And like cattle, and accordingly to raise
The gold-rift naked like the roof-tree gift of magic.

SEIZA
(*Zen position: 'just sitting'*)

The wet leaves smell of hides. Mudskin toad
Under green stars, many brown toads
Sitting in *seiza* like clammy flowers.

The mine chimneys that ventilate the moors,
That moan. In spring, an artist exhalation
From the budding field, the alchemists

101

Are on the move; a bird goes
Sip sip sip; this art of ours,
Balsamic. Under the green leaves

The brown toads full of regard,
In rock-like *seiza*, and full of poison
And red blood, meditators on their

Unused power, warty meditators
Shining slightly in the dark
In *seiza*. The moaning moors,

The rock-houses of the moors which underground
Moan like miners' kine in slantwise winds,
Uncalm, not in rocklike *seiza*, not even

The hollowed mines full of glittering
Upsidedown candles springing from the rock
Arches, seeming stable. An aboveground pig

Shakes its ears out at me honestly
With the sound of shaking out a wet galosh,
And scrutinises me not with piggy eyes

But with the direct black pupils of its lifted nose
Straight as minechimneys. The earth
Snuffs at me, its eyes of hairy lard,

But I am undisturbed, one-pointed,
This snout will be unable to shove me over,
And I should sit in *seiza* for the earth snorts

With an incredible ease, like pulling open
A big pigskin bag. Dark rays blaze
Out of the opening rock, and inside

Unsealed, the clammy flower of rocks,
A smiling toad sitting in *seiza* at the centre,
Unconsumed by nether fires, among

The lowing wind-kine gathering and jostling
Through hollow coal and pastures of crisp quartz,
The moist woods ranked above,

The wet leaves of the forest paths that lie
Like a tannery yard of toadskins,
And the toad sitting in *seiza* who cannot grunt

Even while his skin is stripped, sitting in *seiza*,
Ochre flower of blood, contemplating the mud
That grows a skin of flowers, the limbecs,

The mud like the conjurer's black cloth
Pulled through the seed's ring and flourishing painted,
The toadskin mud sitting hunkered, feathery

With birdtracks and a down of flowers.

THE ALCHEMICAL HONEYMOON
(*Penzance Hotel*)

The fatness of the ocean: the
Opulence of the earth: the groom appears,
The bronze man, so tanned it's green

Or a hint of green, as the folios wish.
The chymical embrace in the bath, the rainbow
Vessel, the foaming bathsalt

Of four colours. The water is a womanly
And gentle star, shaking its light to the embrace.
The honeymoon suite is a little chilly, like a church,

But there are white crystals of light
Sparkling over a slate-dark sea, and there are
Lead masses of cloud in the east at sunset

The dwindling sun projects, and tinges with gold,
As it does the concrete-works on Newlyn shore
White as a mosque and a factory of mosques

Among the darkening sand-dunes, that were gold till now.
I had new glasses for my marriage, and they picked out
The blue objects and the gold ones, especially

The gold tinctured to blue as the shadows grew
And made a whole blue about us, particularly of the dunes
Mirrored in the wet blue beach. But even then

A fire was lighted behind a dune, like a grain
Of virus gold, our cone, our Stone, the dune
Whose summit opened in a door of fire

Tended by a small dark figure at his furnace, an opening door
To jumping blue-gold shadows on an ink-blue shore,
The smoke rising in a crooked tower

Of jagged shade that climbs into the last light
Whose floor it finds, and gilds with it
Until it fades into the black that builds

Upon us, planetarium; and I think,
As I climb towards my bride in the starched evening sheets,
Of the Sinbad who uncorks the genie's prison,

Who steps back on the sands as the smoke
Sparkling with power pours up
Like a reversed waterfall out of the green sea-bottle

Unstoppered by a sailor bronzed
By his travels in the sea's furnace,
Voyager in an Ascot and tailcoat cracking a seal.

THE YOUNG AND PREGNANT SPIRITUALIST

By mere breathing, she sees her own shape,
The solemn tranquillity of her naked life
Under her clothes, the day-long caress.

The tie of each sitter like a crucifix
Nailed to the throat, their heads
Being washed in blackness; she is

Washing their heads with night
In her chant, her moaning chant,
They bow their heads and take it,

All of them, in their circle, the sitters.
She has a baby in her womb that sways in its bonds.
In trance, that baby is, communicating with her;

And she tells herself this child is of such a virtue
I am made a prophetess. Accordingly I speak
From the womb to these nice young chaps

Who serve in country offices and shops;
I help them jump the counter into this world.
The room is psychic, the whole space answering,

The draperies flutter at the windows in grimaces,
Straining to speak, the great sewn faces,
The very air is living with currents like her birthwater,

And tapping out her heartbeat there climbs a disc,
The luminous tambourine, to which there floats
An ectoplasm that grasps the shivering drum

Like a foetus in its robes,
Or like a lily unfolding, and from the draperies
Steps out a spirit naked as pips, with

A few wisps caught up for modesty; and to herself
This is the grown-up image of her baby
Adult and unspoilt; I pray I will meet her

In our afterlife together; but now
She is the centre of this circle, they may ask
Their questions, and to one it is

The dead wife returning, to another
His sainted grandmother, seeing her drapery as age,
Those wisps clinging to the face as wrinkles, but I,

I know she is the future
Growing in me and talking round this table

DUESSA

In this nothingness are hidden hills.
I hear beesong in wall, in well.
I see each grain glinting in the sundial
Packed solid with its thousands of days.
The old train twangles past, the sea falls silent.
The sky pulls itself up to its full height.

She will dress as a kind of spider for the party,
Waistcoat of fur close as a black mouse,
The logo brooch of diamond eyes in sixes sparkling,
Snowflake logo, sheer spiderousness.

In this nothingness are hidden hills
Blue as steel in their distances,
Drawn up to their full height.
There are veils which clothe a mystery,
That do not hide it, but reveal,
As the logo-patterns of her dress,
As the shirt-weave which withers as she turns,
Tautens in its threads as she returns.

She dresses in a white silk shirt
With full sleeves that is her web,
In velvet trousers, waistcoat of black fur,
Mouse-fine and close, and a small silver hand
Clasped in her hair holds unmelting
A snowflake logo of eyes in sixes.

Blessed Duessa with the excited breath
Smelling of hot coins, in her spider-trademark,
And smelling of pine-scented nightbreeze
On which is woven a shirt, which breathes
Which brings the man-moths to her, smelling
Of cedar shaving-waters and soft wood.
She is hunting
In her party-gear and in return
Offers something difficult to tell.

It is not enough to prick the quiff
And flutter off. The fat and idle
Powdery malemoth,
His body-juice is ripe to be transferred,
Or else he would not stagger thus
Heavy into the wheeling web.
The pelvic basin floods.

As the floods recede, some closeness
To another world, greater than this,
Or what we assume is this, that reveals itself
Like a well-known text transforming, returns
As the page turns, its back showing,

And as the dexter page wheels about, it becomes
The sinister one, which is illuminated;
Everywhere the net of jewels starts up in the hedges,
The spider in her hidden alps, her star-shaped clothes,
That dumpling shudders in her Taj Mahal,

And as she steps out of her spider-dress
All the spiders step out of their dresses
To the sound of mist and music, in the party dawn.

107

THE WITCH WHO LOVES US

Their prayers emptied the schools.
The burning witch lighted up the whole wood.
They let the children consume

The entire cottage of gingerbread.
They wanted it gnashed down to the foundations.
The cottage drawers were full of wonderful food.

The little girls and boys
Groped their way to the feast by witch-light.
They gorged themselves by this flambeau

And swore they had been helped to more
By the kind lady with hair aflame
Who smiled on them and heaped handfuls

Crying, my loves, my loves,
And dipped fingers between her ribs
Offering snapdragon raisins and glowing meat

And reached deeper into her bones
Like long conches of delicious marrow
Burning like golden syrup, and the children danced

With the food in their dripping hands and ate
Singing, the witch, the witch
Who loves us, the witch who loves and gives.

Then the grim-jawed men overheard their feast
And grasped that her spirit of fire
Could not be burned, and with

Full bellies and a light
From the witch that lit up the whole soul
Drove the children from her sinking pyre.

THE REASON WHY WITCHES WEAR BLACK

I

For meditation: my alcohol, hops,
Water, glass, paper, fire and tobacco machine.
I dress in black to express a space.
In this pub-dusk I am collar and cuffs
Shining in an empty chair of twilight,
Collar and cuffs and burning paper.

II

The firemen in their hats of brass trumpet
And their hoses of white hiss: the accelerando
Fire composition, hushed *piano* with water improvisations
Of the canvas baton, and the paper factory
Melts in its music, the hoses
Breaking white collars out of the hot stiff charcoal.

III

The moth lay where she had fallen
Off the black glass on to the window sill
At night with her flowery skirts around her head
Her thin black legs kicking like hoses. The women watched,
Then went outside to water the garden,
All their black hems like creepy-crawlies
Trailing them along the paths, perambulating darkness.

IV

She had never felt anything as powerful as her own lassitude,
It was the angel she had to fight, dedicated
To preserving her tenderness in black garb,
Save only that upwards towards the voice
The huge frills of the blouse were rising
In a hollow stair of complication up the bosom,
Pleats of white light in their pomp unfolding
Like the stiff echoes of a snowy shout,

On to the articulate throat, that mountain hut
Above the nursery slopes, where the two worlds meet;
No spot of black ink shall mar that frill
Or blot wrenching those echoes into witchy laughter.

V

But this is why witches wear black, so they shan't be seen
Hoisting the goblins up on sticks in the night-parades,
The pumpkins packed with candlelight moving of themselves,
The green bodies glowing and invisibly their priestesses
Steering the show of the green garden dead, now living
In succulence matured at Hallowe'en, the sacred
Conjuring-trick;
                    like the grain dying and becoming my drink,
The tobacco burning itself into a soothing consultant,
The firemen at improvisation with their quenching water-
    flames,
The long dresses adding their black music to a walk,
The white frills of the tides promenading all night.

AIR

I

Blowing breath at each other,
The air from the inside darkness
Palpitates with the heartbeats,
And it is living air. It is
An invisible quicksilver flowing
Round your fingers as you touch.
Its touch is very great,

It is a diffused flesh, breathed from the warmth
And the darkness inside which is not dark at all,
Any more than the night of stars is dark,
Black, without darkness.

110

II

The dung becomes excellent butters;
The butter is bewitched mud.
The large wind moves with its terrible light and shade
　blowing
Out of the nightside of earth;
The great tapestry flaps; the hawk returns
Safely to the woven soldier's wrist. Blowing
Breath at each other which is not
Vaulted into words, simply
Spinning rooms that are round and of an incense,

And irradiate like electrix, for she grows dreamy
And that tapestry the skin flaps again,
Hung with gorgeous matters, tales and swift images.

III

Trakl uses an unusual word for breath:
Odem. It is his Atmosphere
And his little Sister. There is nothing
More ghostly than breath:
The skin of wind moulded to the hills,
The moulding breeze of the hills,
The birds flocking into the great tapestry,
The rain like bells in an infinite number
All descending on the one note, and on this note
The forms grow green and tall
And give out creative breath,

The forms of the downpour itself grow tall
In the wind that flaps these white tapestries,
White stitched on white-blowing pictures of the world,
White trees taller than trees; through the white forests of
　breath
Soldiers marching to a drum of water in white clothes.

111

TANTRIC FRIENDS
For Su and Alan Bleakley

I

At the moment of little death
A man bursts into sweat as if by sorcery.

II

Now the flames are full of pictures,
Full of television stored solid in the coal.
Dust in the belfry dances as it chimes,
Dust flocks to the bell
Clinging to the electrix generated by its ringing.
Swinging the bell in a magnetic field
Improves its tone.
And the old bell not much rung shakes out gossamer,
The whole nave pulsing with gossamer.

III

The bells sign out the apple-harvest.
Foxwhelp cider apples.
Hangydown oak vats.
The oak is fermenting the apple-tree.
Her vat is fermenting my fruit, our tree.
We are tantric friends. Man is a device
For harvesting the abundant details of the woman,
Woman a busy press of the plain juices of the man.

IV

The cider-feast, the sharp, heady smell;
The knowledge is in the bottle, the knowledge
Of the countryside. The Cider-Master
Has the knowledge, that of blending the two trees,
The fruit of one in the vat of the other.

What comes is a spirit, a liquor of excited juice.
The oak vat, and the oak press, the glittering squeezings,
The tree that ferments the spirit of another tree,
Friends, tantric friends. The Cider-Master
Has the knowledge of marriage, friends.

The child is a spirit, crowned with odour.
His effervescence snaps and sparkles.

V

The stone beds of the press. The harvest
Of yin-force out of the apples, the true crop,
Skimming the tree-crown, making potent love
In the apple-slime. Love makes itself
By ferment.

This love I feel is a yeast, a ferment.
What I have is in the press.

VI

The bells call from the towers.
Torn gossamer floats into my cider, I pick it out,
The magnetic zest between us, the resonance,
As of quiet bells singing faintly
To the sound of distant city bells.

As the nearer churches begin their chases,
Music drips from the iron bells
In heavy chimes like fruit, and the air
Brims with the heady spirit, like cider,
Air crushed by bells to give its piercing spirit.

(The man who died from asexual sorcery
Could not breathe, and therefore fancied
Sorcerers everywhere, who cracked the bells
That shook themselves to bits, his breath
Into too many singing fragments, his belfry lungs

Bled with the crushed air, each puff
Harvested new orchards of apple-cheeked spit.)

The apples roll under the wheeling stone,
Each is a world, with inhabitants.
Like gods, we drink up the apple-world.

FLOW AND FOLD

I

The dead have become a one identical fluid
In the balls of potent men.

You snatch the sheet off the ghost —
There is nothing there. The meaning

Of the ghost is all flow and fold.
There is dry frost everywhere like spirit photos,

Spirit clockwork. The reeds are frosted,
And they blow a glitter into the wind,

Their shells shattering. The sleepy poppy-seeds,
Look at this dry handful of them, each is moulded

Like the light drysoldered heads of the dead.

II

The bee with its snout going down
Like a boy drawing on a lilac stocking.

The flower like a yellow mind
Surrounded by lilac thought.

114

The bee with its snout deep in a lilac flower
Like the mind plunged in its reverie. The meaning

Of this ghost we call a flower is all
Flow and fold. It marks the passing.

It marks the air with perfume
Commanding the bee to its fresh station.

With those same killing secateurs
The spider snips out of its web the trapped bee,

It will not interrupt the flow,
It will not drink this potency,

It profits that they work together.
The web is touched again with chords

Of lenses, like a spirit
Settling and demonstrating music.

CITY OF BOYS

Who was cast out of heaven
But is alive in me. A certain
Ghost dangles foaming in his jaw.

My tongue licks my palate
And the big shed of my jaws
Distils. The head of beer

Pocked like the Moon in craters
Alive in me. In this city of boys
A million open collars of beer

The fizz hanging in the throat
Like a gossamer in a well,
The moon going down

In black tides, the spirit
Distilling in the dark retorts
Coiling behind flat waistbands,

Distilling through the brains
Then leaving them limp
Like a dangling ghost,

Then back to the homes
The heads parade, take off
In sleep like wings, awake

To the resonant crystal
The TV chamber which is square,
The prisoner of light fluttering therein,

And the smell of disapproval
Over her entire skin like a low lawn.
The beer with its collars of light

Turning the gutdark to light,
Sweeping with its short-lived torches
Through twilit gullets. Which

Was cast out of heaven but
Is alive in me. The crystal
Tankards with their

Brilliant ghostly heads; how
The true crystals venerate the candles,
Resound to the exploring light,

Sing to the torch held up
In the great unexpected cave far underground,
The cave with fountains and a river

That casts itself out of heaven
In waterfalls, visible
And invisible falls of light.

BUTCHERS

The butcher's red shop hard by the public rose-garden,
The roses like hacked ends, alas,

The meat blooming, and blood-buds on the sawdust,
Which wasps come to devour and not bees to sip.

The Butcher's of veined slabs and gilt letters,
The hands of butchers so white they need blood

Like plump flour-blooded moths visiting their gardens
Of the roses out of the pigs, the sty-roses,

The white hands running over pigs
Opening lardy buds and rose-sutures.

A savage gothic laugh from the coldstore,
The lusty men of cold steel,

The rapierists swashing good-tempered blades,
The exploding light of the cleavers.

It is asking for it to order a nice leg
Or chicken-breasts in the body-shop;

They pinch it and wink, or what about this then Mam?
Slapping a sausage-length down the cold stone counter.

At his reunion, the butcher's campaign medals
Tinkle like distant bayonets; peering over the park wall

117

The roses like a bombed cloud of spirits,
He snuffs up the perfume of their transformed sweat,

Sausage-fetterer, blood-seedsman,
Scalding his kidney-trays,

Hosing down his freezing slabs at night,
His violet light that butchers flies

Switched off until morning and the dawn of meat,
Or burning through the night, shingle of hygiene.

THE GHOST-BOMB KISS

All the buds of the wood
Like bees settled and trembling.
The dawn

Like a white noise at the edge of the field.
The cruel twist in a month.

She signed the apple-green chit in the game called ombre.

The young horses sprinting through the shade of oak-trees,
Mingling sweet haybreath, hanging up their mists,
Skin-mists and breath-mists.

Stay-behind tricks of all sorts.

The terrorist kisses the grenade,
The crocodilian fragmentation-coat.
The metal is warm in her hand.

The street is sunlit, then bomblit.
Shrapnel and bees of brick whine past,
Ricochet bees.

The ghost-bomb kiss.

How many ghosts flowing from this firebomb seed?
Fire-seeds, drowning the sunlight.
The bomb kisses back.

The fruit that is a door slamming violently.
The bud wrapped in greasy paper like a grenade
The shape and sound of a hive.

The last stay-behind trick.
The game of fire and shadow.
The cruel twist round the fiery corner.

The young horses on fire sprint from under the oak trees
        that are on fire.

PRESENCES

The moon a thin
Bottle of stone full of salt water.

The spider in its lift-cage,
Its salt-white vehicle.

The echoes of wings caught in the web,
The beautiful long-haired corpses of wings,

The shell-thin corpses with the trailing hair
And ribs like salt tide-marks dried in sands.

A hand of bones like a shell-arrangement
Shells of a curious sturdiness, resembling white dice.

Listen to the sea echo in the skull;
The air wanders in currents long and trailing as the hair.

The ice clamps in its contracting glass
Or on the freezing rock that condensed it.

The vast screens of the cement-works
Broken by frost, the powdered bone in draughts

Like light blowing through the gap under the door.
Open the doors, they cast vaster powdery shadows.

The statue-works, turning rock to smoke and presences
Of still people in clouds of settling dust,

Still people among the artisans flickering with their chisels,
Still people whirring on their axis in the lathes

Under the moon spinning on its lathe
The stone cries out

Spinning under the chisel carving ears,
The long hair winds

Of the echoes of cries of the bald white statues.
The still person who is solid shell

Like the sea of zero, whiter
For in the lathes of ice, the presence of salt.

AND HE CAUSETH SOULS TO SHINE BY THEIR OWN
LIGHT

I

The barn full of straw rustling
We were the chunky engine
Working it from our forme;
It was a congregation of sexuals
Invisible ones rustling their silks,

120

Rustling their pages,
And we a cross between electric sparks
And intent readers in many volumes
Of her work printed
On the left-hand pages,
Mine on the right.

II

The rustling of the pilchard through silky tides
My lantern charged with fish-oil, the stinking
Inexpensive seaside-lamp I light
By striking a stone in which there is a woman
Of light, threaded invisibly through the flint;
She leaps and becomes a flame
Which stands up spitting on the smooth oil.

III

The man a lantern of man-oil, shining.
So that he may continue when decedent
To shine he is bathed in natrium,
It converts him to eternals
To lastings like date-coloured longjohns
Packed with long stones fastened
With black fingernail-buttons,
And he will be polished like a precious book
Bound in itself
Its own text, the same potent work
That shines by oil in all the portrait coffins.

IV

It is much the best that he stands like no stone
Carved with his limited dates
While the man fades in the image-drinking soil;
Let him be this herring-colour,
This rich gold that rustles in its wrinkles!

The creamy skull shines through the freckles of age,
Oh longlaster!

V

Silver is the female bone
Because she is said to corrode monthly
But polishes herself up to splendour,
Therefore she may keep eternally shining
In this soft self-leather signifying sex;
The glad embalmer's friction polishes it up to splendour;
Draw the round cup out of the soft pouch,
Drink up the glory!

TOWN AND COUNTRY

I

An eiderdown embroidered with
A thousand sleeping lids;

An eiderdown concrete-hued and sewn
With a hundred thousand windows,

Her town sleep, her country sleep.

II

The flies as the fume of acid sunshine
Consuming the world, fast, pecking it up,
As the spiders tipple at the flies.

She entered — fascinating presence —
Instantly there was an intuition of order.

I thought of the butterfly or soul
Of a man that wanders off when he is sick:
Thus it returns.

III

The sky was brass-coloured.
The traffic rang like trumpets.
The heat wriggled over the slate roofs
Like a plague of serpents.

IV

Under television aerials like
Elaborate can-openers, we sat
By the awakening-tree,

The cherry that was waking up
In the Spring sunshine, wooden construct
Of a thousand sleeping lids
Like the knots or eyes in wood
Getting themselves soft lids
So they could know awakening; this despite

The brass-sounding air, the roar of cars.
In the paddock, the violin-faced horse
Trotted over, his nostrils music.

The muzzle of that wolf, the wind,
Tattered the blossoms.

III

There was the almost-silent work,
The spring of water, continuing
Under the threshold of sleep.
I thought of the little rivers
Of ghosts there, of the spirits
Who in nightmares rattled tambourines
As if they were chains.

IV

Now we were drinking up our beer
In a pavilion with green curtains blowing,
The wind and rain worrying at the tent,
Our clothes embroidered with eyes, some open
And some closed, depicting the wind, the flowers.

ANOTHER YOU

Anyone who is naked
Or taking a bath
Is to the child a baby.
And the child
Reminds the man
Of a former lover, since
That lover was attempting to conjure
The child of her flesh
Out of a man, any
Suitable man, whose
Phallus was the generator
Her place the manifester;
Any child reminds him,
With its sayings
And clear assumptions.

Separated from you
By the glass of your eyes,
The pelt of your skin,
And now the ramparts
Of your journey, since
The tilting plane
Taking you distant
Scoops a great rubble of sunset
And in the sunset
A great rubble of sound.

The dew smoking away white
In jagged clouds, the dew
That was like lanterns of electrix
On their green cables; the thin
High razor-scream of the leading edges
Of the gull's wings as they cut
The seamless air, like silk
Screaming; and the journeying planes,
They drone at the tip of their great
Showering sound like thirty-thousand-foot-
Tall burdoun pipes of an improvising
Organ that travels over the ground;
I stand at the base of this note

In the icy air, the air
Full of razors, the puddles
Full of ferny knives. In the warm house
I remove your clothes and call you baby.

Pleats breaching the skirt, silk
Intricacies whistling as they go
Shifting and recreating patterns
Over the skin like a mirror of solid
Reflections, a certain playback
Of your morning assemblage reversed,
A succession of glidings and removals,
The tight clothes focussed on the fork in rays;
Now we relax that complex of indications,
Our meridians or the invisible seams of our flesh
Streaming with the aroused energies;
How the clothes model the underneaths!
The velvet jacket the relaxed skin,
The silk shirt the inner glitter,
The bunched tie a model of the puff
Of perfume escaping into my face
As I pull the loop and the masks collapse.

WORKING WINDOW

I

At the window furious whispering
Of soft voices. Who are the ones
That can turn on the rain that it may descend
In pleats and bundles,
February violets?

II

A slow drumming
Out of the black ships huddled on the water;
I heard this in her shadow.

III

But all the masterpieces join up behind themselves
In this body of the world
Radiant with moving streams,
With ashless fires. I did not want

IV

To go with this girl Jane
In her silks and flowing shifts,
It would be too smooth an investiture,
But it was not, it was

V

Not, for the masterpieces joined.

VI

The beautiful jewelled shirt of wheels
Falls from all its trees, the tides
Fold to and fro in this lantern

Which is a workshop window, which
Is a room with a bed. The rain

VII

Is hewing at the seed, the wheel of rain
That spins inside the woman (through the curtains
A glimpse of that great circuit of the water
Spinning its drops and webs;
I part the cloth and enter
The wheel of our species,)

VIII

The rain
Becoming sweeter-tasting as it falls, and sweeter
As the season draws on, for all the pollens,
Nectars, honeys, rising perfumes store
In this rainbody that wheels above,
Swoop down in furious soft voices
At this working and whispering window.

THE SHIPS

I

There are two genders, human and brute,
Not counting the high caste
Or major gender, of gods.

II

Her belly, her bread-basket
Smells of fresh bread.
I lie beside her
Inhaling this produce ever-fresh.

127

III

I lie within her planetarium, its domed roof
Repeats the picture-code of night,
Calls down an astrology on its occupant,
Child or man; it is like a mine
Of sequent chambers penetrated
With one's light held high,
Of increasing conductivity and lustre,
Lead, tin, iron, copper, mercury, silver, gold,
Showing their lights in our skins, sequentially.

IV

Now we rise to assume
The terrible false town-and-country rictus,
Like smiling ghosts
Issuing from the sailing world of the sheets.

V

As we walk to the school by the harbour,
And the elements balance on this walk,
There librates on the water the soul-image of a cutler,
The spirit of the great knifemaker incarnate in a ship,
The ship called *Master-Cutler* made of the substance of
    knives.
There are many ships on this water manned,
Like castles floating on their knife-edge.
We are glad

VI

The prison-ship has quitted our harbour
Which smelt of cocoa, chlorine and ironing
And men turning to stone
Smelling of sweat and chocolate, but

VII

The shores are lined with thousands of homes like prisons
Flickering with the light from a stone,
The false phosphor that petrifies of television;
They are turned away, and show their backs

VIII

To the ethers of the sailing-vessels,
The sitz of their planks and crackling linen,
The ships of high caste
Quitting the harbour of brutes.

THE OFFICES IN THE OLD BATHS
For Peter Porter

I

The maroon-hued slugs swallow the garden down.
Out at sea the ships on fire with light
Like burning soldiers drawn up on parade.

I switch on the electric light;
It is a furnace in a vase.
Then the maroon that slaps the night:

The lifeboat is out,
One of those lighted ships is toiling
With some current like a great maroon dragon;

Let its stacked lights not be quenched.
I fear some outlying storm is killing men.
In the morning a wheat field

Like a festival of plumes,
Stuffed with wind like lurkers and shifters.

129

II

Our new offices have just been opened in the old Baths,
A clean airy series of halls
In which the paperwork partakes of the cleanness,

And office work is no longer onerous,
Especially on still days
When we can slant the long verandah windows open.

The river sliding past the orchard tastes of apples,
Clean-tasting apple-water.

III

She polished up her hair with the palms of her hands,
Our Chief, and settled back, sighing;
The named constellations overhead, floating,

And the names of the ships bearing their own lights
Through the water of white documents in the dry Baths,
Their own patterns, bearing their own names,

Their own frequencies, *White Sun*,
Rainsource; and the great ships
Which are stars

Drenching us with their light,
The rilling wake, signalling,
The enormous radio operators tapping out,

IV

One of their messages being this cinnamon
I taste in our lunchtime baked apples,
One of the constellations of the odours of Venus,

The multitudinous odours
Knotted into the cold baked apples in the sandwich box.

V

Our Chief slid her scalpel on to the next task;
Uncanny pleasure moved within her.
In her grip she had the lading papers

Of the great barquentine *Mozart*
Just as that magic equipage moved so slowly
Past the broad windows of our offices

Our new offices in the old Baths.
Uncanny pleasure moved within her like a full-rigged ship
As if she entered her naked self

Into a silky sea of ships;
Great full-masters sailed across her breasts.
Her smile in the office means the tide is full,

The draught sufficient,
As the great barque in its weathered colours
Glides past the window, pennant flying,

In its weathered colours.

VI

'When they brought the General home,'
She remarked, glancing at the *Mozart*'s manifest,
'The coffin that had been furnished

Was too small. "May we," asked the men
Charged with the task of burial,
"May we break the General's bones?"

And were almost lynched for this enquiry.
Eventually,' she said, 'He travelled on an open bier,
Two sailors on the deck constantly on guard

To keep the seabirds from his eyes. When
They docked, the salt spray had tarnished almost black
The braid of his dress uniform, and

His dead face was handsomely tanned.'

VII

Dark sails against the light showed the approach
Of a big ship. It was indeed,
As his papers said, the great barquentine

Mozart, with its sails composed
Like a palladian mansion of shuttered light and opening
    shadow.
Would there be

In some inner berth or cabin
Of the great floating house
Of harmonising and motive breezes

Laid on a fleece in this ship
Scrubbed immaculate to its planks,
A new-born child

Stripped of its primordial clothing,
That is to say its Mother,
Who has walked away singing

To drink cordials in another cabin,
Knowing the godlet to be safe now,
Ready to be brought in through the Customs

Into the little seaside town
As the epagomenal days draw in?
There is a flash from the entire sea as the sun goes down;

What will that gliding sun bring
With a hull heavy like a drop of honey, shouldering
Its way through those hexagonal reefs of stars?

VIII

On the lawn outside the Baths
A young horse has got free of its paddock,
Is cantering around, being chased

By a young girl with a bridle,
Our Chief's single-parent family's daughter.
The pony tosses its wet mane

In the sunlight and cracks
Round itself and the child
A rainbow out of the air,

And allows itself to be caught and led at her hand
As at anchor, as if tending to an anchor.

THE HARMONY

I

A storm-cloud like blue-black cliffs
Of a land which is all chasm
Pouring with waterfalls,

A county-sized cloud,
Condenses suddenly,
The first drop flies in like a tear into a skull

The cobweb the skeleton-target, shivering,
All that has shrunk
Its glitter poured into a cobweb,

The glitter stands in the hedges
Like the ghost of the hedges,
The rain falls into all the hedges in its spider-pattern,

The round ladders,
The necklaces that wear the spiders,
The great circuit closed

By the shining knife-switch of the rain,
The spin of the water held quite still in a web
As though the rain were made merely of wheels,

Wheels of water in all the hedges,
Phantom carriages,
Every hedge like a crazy machine of stopped cogs,

A clock with water-wheels,
As though all the rivers had stopped suddenly,
As though the circus of the air had paused

And the mechanism stands shamelessly exposed
Freezing in the snowstorm full of wheels,
Of gossamers,

The spider frozen in his web
The signet of a crazy ladder
His round icicle like a crack on the lake.

II

The tree-sap smells of the green river
On whose bank it grows, the river
Is tributary to the wood,

The treeflowers smell of the melon-tasting river,
The apples are juiced with it,
The fruit and flowers distil the river-water

Like dangling alembics
Each tree in its ancient chemistry
A great green lighted laboratory,

Console or cinema organ of scented chemistry.
The flying magpie
Opens a dark door in the laboratory and passes through.

III

The trees like dogs will proffer themselves
To the richman's lawns,
Lapping with their green tongues,

Perfuming his open window with their flowers
As the dog perfumes his hearth,
So dogs and trees give harmony at the hearth

With their perfumes,
And the cat preens with her audible note,
The dog licking comfortably his sexual flower,

The tree sitting up on the lawn outside
Like a green dog with its cascading paws
Its roots and rootlets riddling to the cellars,

Sipping at the barrels, perfuming them,
Adding its youthful bouquet to the ancient wood,
Reaching behind the masterpieces and the panelling,

And as the masterpieces do, connecting up behind the
    world,
And the young daughter becomes the lover of its balsams,
It glitters outside

Like a piece of the river pausing on its shores,
And like a flower of water the richman drinks
The perfumed current from its leaden bark.

IV

She shelters from the rain
Under the rose-bushes
But is still drenched

135

And laughing and blushing like the roses,
Shaking barbaric water-beads.
In the dusk I ferry her across,

Smooth oars feathering the reflectings.
The willows pore over their river-shadows,
Having fallen into the rain, each emerges

Dressed in one of the rain's million garments;
Drop by drop returns it
To the one garment of a million droplets.

V

The crack of gunshots in the sunlit dawn.
A web between roses like a visible gunsound,
The spider hurtling towards you.

The rose a little scented oven of meditation
With petals wheeling in their flames
And yellow bread baking at the centre.

The pond of glowing orange fish,
A pond like a stone cauldron of molten metal,
The little sunflames stopped at the round parapet

Like moving glances stopped in a stone face.

VI

The birds studded inside and out
With the bolted seeds of their flight,
Unable to bear it

Burst in full-blooming bushes
Like shell-bursts of green
That trace flowering tendrils in mid-air

And gently billow to earth.
All the seeds set in the flight path
Of a bird's life

Build up a green body of enormous volume,
The bird we see
Is one winged hand of this body,

And a beak of this body
Stropping its sticky seeds in chimney-stacks,
Padding gutters with mousy mosses,

Printing green clawsteps down the ancient slates;
And the scullers slide their slender shell
To the murder-voiced coxswains

Down the river and fill its shores
With a green-brown feather echoing from their planks.
What bird, of which this great river is a feather?

The tree-hued bird,
Round wings whirred everywhere.